Touch beyond your reach

Edna Hardaman

ISBN 978-1-957582-00-9 (paperback)
ISBN 978-1-957582-01-6 (eBook)

Copyright © 2021 by Edna Hardaman

All rights reserved. No part of this publication may be reproduced, distributed, or transmitted in any form or by any means, including photocopying, recording, or other electronic or mechanical methods without the prior written permission of the publisher.

Printed in the United States of America

THIS PAGE IS DEDICATED
TO: U.S.
CONGRESSMAN JOHN LEWIS

WE LOVE YOU
AND SHALL ALWAYS REMEMBER
YOUR CONTRIBUTION TO THE CIVAL RIGHTS MOVEMENT
AND TO ALL AMERICA
YOUR VOICE SHALL LIVE ON
BLESSINGS

A TRIBUTE TO THE GREAT U.S. CONGRESSMAN,

CONGRESSMAN LEWIS

FOUGHT AN EXORDINARY FIGHT IN HIS LIFE TIME,
AND WILL ALWAYS BE REMEMBERED
IN OUR HISTORY,
HIS FIGHT WAS FOR ALL AMERICANS
TO BE THE BEST, AND SHARE EQUAL RIGHTS.
ALSO, TO LIVE, LOVE, AND RESPECT ONE ANOTHER.
MOST OF ALL LEARN HOW TO ACCOMPLISH THAT MISSION.
FARE WELL AND GOD BLESS.

THIS PAGE IS DEDICATED

IN HONOR OF RUTH BADER GINBURG
U.S. JUDGE

U.S. SUPREME COURT

2020

THIS PAGE IS IN OUR TIME (2020)

THIS IS PAGE IS IN HONOR OF: George Floyd

Just say a silent prayer

GOD BLESS EVERY ONE

THIS PAGE IS DEDICATED TO ALL THE "SONS"
ACROSS THE WORLD!
FROM ALL "MOMS"
(In my opinion)

When you turn to say goodbye, I may be unable to reply,
To you, but you shall know the reason as to why?
But my mark shall be there.
When, you come to gently knock on my door,
There may not be an answer, but my mark shall be there.
When you begin to dial my number on your phone,
There may not be an answer,
But my mark shall be there.
As you gently walk down the street, and look back to say,
Ha, or goodbye, there may not be a return,
As to why?
But my mark shall be there.
You shall remember giving me a hug, thus saying
Hello or good bye for that particular day.
It shall be then; you realize the simple reason why?
Because my mark shall be there.
I desire for you to know, my mark shall take my place,
And you shall remember, the direction I suggested for you to go.
However, when that time shall come, stop and

MY MARK IS (continued)

Think of those precious moments that unfold
In your HEART.
They shall take my place.
Because my MARK, shall be with you.
Forever, for a memory that shall always live.
LOVE.

"WONDER"

As we wonder, entering into a new year, 2021,
We cannot begin to fathom, and answer the question:
What is next in line or what is on our wondering mind?
Where do we attempt to go from here?
And how do we get to our own arrival?
As we wonder, what is waiting for us?
These times, have a horrendous effect on our mind.
As we try to cope with these turbulent times,
So again (we wonder)?
Because this is a cause and effect on all mankind.
Yet we may think, WE THE PEOPLE.
As we wonder within a quiet moment of rest,
We do not hear a sound, not even a whine from the
Northern winds as they approach us in our silent moments.
Allowing us time to think, obviously, what is next?
Knowing, what is now or what is the next best, choice
To make?
We look, we see, and it is amazing with in our ability,
Yet to be transparent in the process of life.
Because, we wonder?
We continue to touch, to feel, to cry, to hurt, and

WONDER (continued)

To share the inner pain of others.
Because, deep within our heart we care.
your burdens we, also bare,
As we search for, what may be gold,
As the next story begins to unfold,
Day after day.
YES, WE CONTINUE TO WONDER on this forever
turning globe, not stopping for a second,
To rest.
And as for us on this planet, we must continue on
Our journey, not to stop loving, caring, respecting,
Our fellow man and mankind.
In time, (in my opinion)
Time shall be our healer, and together, everyone
Shall figure out the answer to this equation,
In our life and reveal the inside scope of our unknown.
We must hold on to hope, as we, continue
TO WONDER?

A change
"THE CAPTURE OF A SPECIAL KISS"

A special KISS, in the moment of bliss, offered me,
A special change in my life.
I remember when I was a young teen, one HOT
Afternoon, on a SUMMER DAY,
Suddenly, I looked up and saw a friend coming my way,
as he became closer to me,
I could barely see a smile on his funny face,
My body became numb, at the time, I wanted to run,
However, my feelings got in the way,
I thought immediately, I can't allow him to get away.
As he approached me and held out his hand,
I gently begin to stand, and offered a smile.
Suddenly, without delay, he gently pulled me closer his way.
My mind, became stunned, as what next to say?
So, I became silent, as a quiet moment in the stillness of the night.
A slight kiss, was offered to me, as I gently entered his arms,
I suddenly offered my tender and innocent charm.
But at the same time, I knew, to gently move from his
Remarkable, arms, and in so doing.
I felt safe and secure.
However, this moment, brought me a special

Peace, I had not experienced before.
Knowing in the moment of bliss,
A special kiss, could last for evermore.
I shall never forget that special,
HOT SUMMER DAY.

"EACH DAY"

Each day is a new and GLORIOUS DAY!
A day we have not seen,
A day we have not lived,
But another day GOD has granted us to share and give
To others.
Another day the sky has opened, for us to see.
You and me!
Another day the clouds are woven together as one
Hugh blanket to protect us.
Another day, of joy and happiness,
And maybe a little sorrow added to our day,
But one thing for certain!
We, know GOD loves all of his children.
And, FATHER GOD, WE THANK YOU, AND LOVE YOU TOO.
AMEN!

"EYES"

The sparkle in your eyes, match the stars in the sky.

I wonder what exactly, do they think??
When they look back, and attempt to blink
At you.
Guess?
Might I be, describing
Your eyes or the stars?
Both are beautiful.

"INVISIBLE TOUCH"

In the comfort of myself, I feel an invisible touch,
Whispering, oh, how I love you so much!
In the comfort of myself, I gently offer a respond,
Unknown to others, this is just for us.
In the comfort of myself, I smell the sweet fragrance,
Built with in the secret of our love,
In the comfort of myself,
I make an attempt to take a breath to stay alive for you.
And for our most intimate moments we share.
Because our, love shall always, be attached. As a chain linked together
As ONE.
In the comfort of myself.

"MAKE ROOM FOR ME"

Please, I asked you, make room for me,
Because, I am coming home, to my surprise.
Because, things I had planned has not materialized,
For example,
I had big dreams, for myself.
Dreams of my future, such as my education plans,
Good jobs, a nice home, and all that goes with
A dream?
However, I have learned in my efforts, try, try, again.
So, I need a new start, and I am on my way home.
And reality of true life,
And to never look back, when the going gets tuff.
Oh, I have learned so much in my struggle these past years.
Perhaps, now I can see the light,
And search for a new start.
I have decided to come home and never more to roam.
Because my place is this humble and incredible
Place called HOME SWEET HOME.
THANKS TO YOU.

"A SLIPPERY PATH"

Sometime our feet slide off the trail, we are walking on.
But there is a mighty force, pulling us back to our
Proper place.
And we begin to recognize, we are at the beginning
Of our trail, once again,
We try to hold on firmly, in that moment.
So, we begin to pray for the strength to hold on, one
More time.
If we slip, we hope our feet will hold to
The solid rock, on which we now stand.
And for ever hold to GOD's unchanging hand.
When we think back, the slippery path was fun,
But only when we were very young.
We took the chance, on that slippery path,
But a slippery path shall not last,
We now have learned, over the years, to
Hold on tight with all our might,
Because chances are, somehow if we may fall,
We pray, GOD BLESS YOU, ONE AND ALL.
Please, stay on the solid rock,
To avoid your unseen fall.

"BEING PREPAIRED AND BEING READY"

To me, being prepared, is making preparation,
Having the ingredients for any given situation,
At the time, of your thought process.
To be prepared, everything must be at hand,
To begin the next step.
Of course, the process is in the plan of action,
Proceeding forward, with one's plan,
Please keep in mind,
"preparation"

BEING READY, IS THE anticipation, or
Expectation and prediction of an event or a deep rooted
Feeling with in the heart.
A feeling to fight with the strength, and the inter ability
To win the battle, to be won, upon the face of time.
Because, time is ticking away, minute, by minute.
Time does not wait, it does not come to a halt,
Because it is Time.
With that being said, I think it calls for RESPECT.

BEING PREPAIRED/ BEING READY (cont.)

Being ready, provides an inter
Feeling of peace at best.
Ready for the great dreams, that may or may not come true,
Ready for the down falls as well, that may interfere,
With plans, or reality.
However, I think, the spiral pattern of life takes its place for a purpose.
That purpose is: to be ready and prepared.
For whatever LIFE throws your way.
Now you have a great and wonderful day.

"A CRACK IN THE WALL"

Ha, watch out, there is a crack in the wall.
Wonder why that crack is there?
And wonder what purpose does it serve, or
What message does it relay?
And most of all who is it for?
Is it a sign of peace, joy, and happiness? Just
take a look, it appears strange.
It is not very long in size, nor is it,
Very wide.
On the other hand, it may have a story to tell.
Just look at it,
If it had the ability to speak to us,
I, wonder what it could say? To us.
I feel it is a sign of safety, joy, good health, and peace.
Look at it closely, it appears to be an
Outline of JESUS ON THE CROSS.
YES, that is our answer, as to why it is there.
And that is the story it is sharing with us,
To release a FEELING, WE ARE BLESSED.
Now, I feel no fear, because this is a sign
JESUS IS HERE for all to dwell in the house of the LORD.

"HAPPINESS IS BEING FREE"

Take a deep breath, and for some reason, one feels free.

A deep breath of freedom, in my opinion, creates
A great relief to the soul, you may give vent to your feelings,
And receive a gift of reassurance to your life.
Many people need to vent in this day and time.
On the other hand, a gift to oneself, is the greatest
Gift of all.
To have the ability to, talk, walk, and think of what makes you happy?
Each individual deserves the opportunity to be happy
And free, I think this is a special prize to oneself.
I also think this brings a sense of tranquility to one's life.
Just to sing, dance, be joyful, to love, to be loved,
This gives reason just to care about others.
Actually, freedom has provided that moment
Just to become free, it helps us to see, what is
Before us.
Such as: the clouds over head, above the clouds
Thru the clouds around the clouds, under the clouds
And most of all, the movement of the heavenly clouds
In a sense, the clouds are a free element.

"LOOK"

Stop and look in front of you, exactly what do you see.
A sunny day, a gloomy day, a cold day, a hot day,
Or allow me to guess? Just another day?
That GOD HAS KEPT YOU IN HIS ARMS OF MERCY.
Allowing you to see, a tree top, a bird fly, just passing by
To say hello with its chirp, on that day
What about a beautiful flower garden?
Or masses of people just gazing.
For example, some laughing, some crying, some living,
And some dying. This is a sad time for everyone,
Oh, what a day, captivating our attention, on all of these things.
Maybe good or maybe sad, but somehow, we must
Try to live for tomorrow, and accept whatever may come your way.
Just give someone, something,
You shall remember on the next day.
STAY FOCUSED IN FRONT OF YOU.
JUST LOOK!

"OH! MY BRAIN IS WORKING OVER TIME"

Oh, my brain is working overtime, because of
What I see, and hear, my poor brain is taking it all in.

Wait! for a moment I think, my brain is over loaded,
And working overtime. But why??

I think the reason is because it is hearing a lot of confusion
And added complexity, to the stories I hear, yes, the stories I really hear.
Now, I see trouble coming, running with its' paint brush, coming
Toward me, attempting to paint an ugly picture.
A picture that is unacceptable. But for all to see.
However, trials and tribulations are causing my brain
To work over time, without slowing down.
Now I am wondering how I shall make an attempt to go forward.
But something must give, some relief must come.
Surrender, must come to rescue the TRUTH.
The race of time is near, so I must hear, the
The silent tone of MERCY!
But I must be still! In order to hear.
this act of mercy, and maybe my brain shall slow down,
and relax a bit. And I shall pray reality, will
come in time to create a change.
For me and everyone.

"OUR TIME IS AS ONE"

I want to share with you, on today, your time is also my time.
Oh, my darling, I love you so much.
Your kiss, your smile, your soft voice, but most of all,
I love your tender, tender touch.
When we meet, I feel chills on my entire body,
As when winter snows bring a blizzard in winter time.
I also become speech less without words, to say,
Because, I tend to freeze in my own tracks,
And my entire body becomes numb in that moment.
I lose my ability to respond,
Because your beauty has my mind captivated.
It is like I am in another world, that goes without saying.
Your sweet fragrance, captivates the air, and
Reality becomes like a dream, in paradise.
When we spend time together, and I hold your
Young and tender body close to mind.
That moment indicates to me,
Your time is my time,
And together, we become one.
The equation equals our time together forever.

"A SHORT STORY OF BACK IN THE DAY AS I REMEMBER IT" (GOOD OLD DAYS)

This little story is about an old iron cook stove, and the old days.
Begins like this
Years ago, I remember very well the site of the old-time iron cook stove,
At my grand ma's house, however this old iron stove is best described
As an old wooden cook stove, it even had a side door,
That was the oven area for baking a delicious cake or strawberry pie.
This is the reason why, I am sharing with you, my readers.
Those old cook stoves were a site to see as in amazing.
I recall my grand ma's old cook stove and how a meal
Was prepared in that day and time.
She prepared the fresh vegetables such as cabbage, potatoes, beans,
Greens and a large slab of country ham, and don't
Forget the corn bread made from scratch,
It was cooked in the oven part of the old cook stove.
And some time a sweet potato pie was a treat to eat.
Having been prepared from that old cook stove.
But it tastes so good to me.
This old wood burning cook stove burned chopped wood
In the top area of the stove, yes, someone had to chop
Real wood to perfectly fit inside this old stove.

(short story continued) GOOD OLD DAYS

There were iron plates that fit on top of the wood burning stove
And this was the location for the pots of vegetables to cook.
(in other words, they were lids).
And they were HOT to the touch.
After the old stove was REALHOT, my grand ma was ready
To cook that delicious meal for all to enjoy
Every little girl and boy.
When the entire meal was ready, grand ma would
Call everyone to EAT, and it was a treat for all.
In those old times the meals were absolutely
Good and tasty.
I always enjoyed BREAKFAST most of all because,
My mom prepared hand made
Biscuits and fresh strawberries from the fields,
(Strawberry fields). Someone had picked them.
Of course, we were on our summer vacation from
Northern Indiana.
So again, this life style was all new to me,
But I learned how to cope as a child.
And I enjoyed the food.
My job was to wash the dishes after each meal,

(short story continued) GOOD OLD DAYS

And that was an entirely different story.
Someone had to pump the water from the old pump
On the outside porch.
Grand ma had an old aluminon bucket
To contain the cold water from the pump,
My grand pa, in those days build the pump house.
He was a carpenter and a MINISTER. (True story.)
And I was seven years old when he passed away.
I became very sad, because I loved him,
I went everywhere with him on our visits,
Every summer, from Indiana.
My grandparents were very SPECIAL TO ME,
As all grand children see their grandparents.
(Thru the eyes of a child.)
Most of the time I enjoyed the time at their home,
I was free as a bird
I could run and play, each and every day.
Some time with new friends I met,
Along the way.
My favorite time of year was the HOT SUMMER TIME,
Of course, in those days without AIR CONDITIONING,

(short story continued) GOOD OLD DAYS

So, when the weather was REAL HOT, I choose to
Eat ice cubes and popsicles to cool me off.
The only fan available was a fan made from paper,
Keep in mind, this was back in the day,
As we say in these times.
And a paper fan came from the CHURCH,
That had been ordered thru the mail
For the CHURCH.
At that time, a little country church in the village,
Where my grandparents lived.
I also recall walking with my grand pa to visit
Friends in the village, there were not many cars
So, walks were proper in those days.
I liked to walk; it was fun to me in those days.
I must admit, things were not convenient.
I learned to accept the good and the not so good,
It contributed to my experiences as a child.
I have stored these experiences in my
Memory bank, to cherish forever.

"THE ENTER HEART"

The inner HEART, may create a special spark,
Within our mind, at the appropriate time.
Our heart holds many feelings, some time,
We are not aware of our thought process,
Such as burdens, love, sorrow, and despair,
And our heart allows us to be aware, it is always there.
Our heart, must be a place of comfort, respect and love.
And deliver peace to our individual soul,
In order to continue our task in life.
We must develop the feeling in our HEART, to
Share with others, and most importantly,
Always create a special love, toward our fellow man.
We endeavor to make life the BEST it may be
With our own effort at work.
It may be then; we are able to become flexible
In our experiences, of ups and downs,
In the world we are attempting to share.
One thing we do know, our HEART IS ALWAYS THERE.
(in my opinion) our efforts begin with in our HEART.

"UNDER THE UMBRELLA"

LIVING UNDER THE UMBRELLA, I think, it is interesting,
Just because, if there is no rain in sight, why an umbrella?
Here is how my story begins,
I call it GOD'S UMBRELLA!
Because it is invisible to the human eye.
But I see him gently holding it over us, to protect us,
Without our knowledge, of course.
Just stop and think about it, he is keeping us,
From the mighty storms, rain, sleet, and snow
As we come and go, on our daily task.
However, he stretches his umbrella far and wide,
Keeping us by his tender side,
The side, wounded long ago, as none other,
But this tender side is our safety zone, some time we are unaware,
Yet, to remember, the burdens we must bear.
Obviously, we need to think, some time? where did our protection,
Fit in our own situation?
But when GOD' UMBRELLA is held high and wide,
Over our very being, again, it is to our surprise,
And that is a good experience in real life.
To know HE is always there, holding his HEAVENLY UMBRELLA,
For our protection.

"AN Unforgettable LOVE STORY"

Allow me to share my love story with you.
It begins like this:
Have you ever felt love? I am sure you have,
But not like the story I am attempting to share,
In my own words:
My love extends beyond the heart,
Meaning:
I love in the midnight hour, and I love in the early dawn.
I love before the breaking of another unforeseen day.
I love when the stars twinkle,
I love behind the ugly wrinkle of time.
In love when the energy is with me.
I love when I am weak and tired.
I love when the raging storm clouds roar in the
Heavenly bodies above, I love.
I love when (you) might say? I am ok!
I love when your heart beats faster, then
The hands on any clock saying tick tock.
I love when trouble rise,
I love when my heart cries, about you!
I love beyond the distant skies.
I love over the mountain peaks.

LOVE (continued)

I love in the valley so low.
I love as you stop, and I love as you go.
I love when smiles are on your face.
I love when the frowns are unclear, to me and
They seem to be out of place.
I love when you are far away,
Because I love you each and every day.
In my (simple and frantic way).
I love in every twist and turn; I love when life appears very stern.
I love thru the ups and downs.
I love when trials are level with the ground.
I love when you talk, I love when you are silent as the midnight air,
When you look up, to see me standing there.
I love you when your ideals are greatest of all
But, when they do, not work out,
I am there to catch your fall, because I love you.
I love!
Just remember, my love is on the line, and it shall
Live on and never disappear, you shall always be able to feel my love,
Where ever you may go whatever you may do!
You shall know I will always follow you. I am molded in your heart. I LOVE!

"TEARS"

Every tear that is shed, may be signs of hope and joy to come.
Every tear you feel drop, try to catch it, and hold on to it.
Tears are shed, for some to be wiped away
And some time tears wait for the very next day.
Again, sometime tears, stop by to say hello.
Some will come and some may go.
Tears some time may be defined as, enhancing the spirit.
Tears may just leave an unexpected trail.
Tears may allow the future to be unveiled.
Tears do not cost, but someone pays later in life.
A tear may drop into a cup of tea, on that day,
It was meant to be.
Just think about it?
What creates a tear?
For example, a smile, a laugh, distance in a mile?
It may be far and it may be near, one thing we know,
A TEAR IS A TEAR!
A tear may come before you weep, and simply
Disappear while you sleep.
REMEMBER A TEAR IS A TEAR.
However in the end, wipe away the tears!
There is a better day coming, for additional TEARS.

ARIZONA BREEZE

The Arizona breeze, is like nothing you have ever felt before,
Just catch your breath, and I shall tell you more
Before I gently attempt to close the door.
As I sit quietly, and feel the gently breeze,
It brings me comfort and a moment of peaceful ease.
Not to think, nor to blink an eye, but only to sit and
Rest a bit, under the blanket of deep blue skies,
Providing a swift and serene moment of pleasure
Combined with secrets thoughts, unable to measure,
By any time, piece imaginable.
When you think about the gentle breeze,
It has no worries, in this life, so I think in my mind?
And ask the question? What brings you by?
I only thank that gentle breeze that calms the inner soul.
I am unable to touch that breeze, but yet able to feel
The swiftness of its flow.

GOD'S TENDER TOUCH

God's tender touch is ever lasting, IN my opinion.
Because I think one must make a connect with him,
Within the Holy Spirit.
He is listening and waiting for our connection with him.
It may be created, in ways unknown to us, such as
In a dream, a soft voice, and maybe a vision.
However, we shall know by his power and
His grace and mercy.
Because, he knows, how much we can bear in our struggle
In this life.
He knows our problems deep within our soul.
Only, we shall feel his special touch, and then
We shall know his holy will for us!
We shall receive his message, no matter how it may come.
We shall identify, to his love for each and every one.
When we receive GOD'S HOLY TOUCH.

HAND IN HAND

Our hands meet, and our faces greet, but
Our body goes our separate ways!
Who is to say, hello my dear, we have not met in days?
As I remember, we were always,
Walking HAND IN HAND.

"PUSHING THRU DISAPPOINTMENTS"

When disappoints come to visit you, keep them at the door.

Because on the next note, there are plenty more.

Don't allow a disappointment to settle in your brain.
Unfortunately, the next moment shall not be the same.
Put your thought process in a positive mode, and think of your
Next moment, being a successful one alone.
However, when it arrives, you may start over,
Once again.
So, pushing thru disappoints, may be your success,
It is not the end.
Think of preforming your talent, skills, and knowledge.
GOD SHALL PREFORM THE REST.
However, HE asks of you, to preform your very best.

"SWEET AS A PEACH"

Sweet as a peach on a tree, just imagine a beautiful
Peach tree, with peaches hanging high and low.
Do not forget the colors, all array, of red, yellow, and gold.

You may look up or down to find a pretty peach,
Maybe even on the ground,

Some may be big and some may be small
But the question is? Which one is the sweetest?
Of them all.
One thing remains, we know there is a peach tree, there
For you, and for me.
And at the end of day, we must be as sweet as
A peach on a tree.

DON'T WAIT UNTIL THE SUN GOES DOWN

Don't wait until the sun goes down,
You have no time to play.
Be serious, in making your goal in life,
You are not here to stay.
have your goal and purpose too, every moment counts.
Do not set aside today, you need to step to the plate.
Because, some time in life, you will make an out!
Be sure you are careful, and polite.
And share your forgiveness before the darkness of the night.
Look to the WEST, the sun is going down,
you must hurry, to forgive, so you shall
Continue to have a good life to live.

"MY WOUNDS"

"Looking back, over the years, I have suddenly felt,
The wounds of long ago, that once were inflicted, upon me.
And my very soul.
But I dare to say, how I carried those wounds, many years.
However, no one felt, or seen my true pain.
In those years, long ago.
And to say the least, others did not really know.
I covered my wounds for days on end,
Keeping the secret deep within.
(my heart).

Yet, I carried a smile upon my face, none other to take my place.
YES, just being a mere child, at that time.
Those wounds, detailed the scares on my tender body.
Just to remember those days of old, has made me,
Strong and bold.
Only my heart and soul, know
The entire story, as the present pages of time,
Tend to unfold,
In this hidden book of chronological time,
These pages are safely stored in my remarkable mind.
Just a message to my reader, where there is,
A will there is a way. I am a living testament, (GOD HAS MADE A WAY).

"SEEING THE EYES OF JESUS"

Anything worth having is worth the challenge to receive it.
Anything worth getting is a challenge to get it.

Seeing the eyes of JESUS, STRETCHING out his hand to us,
Is a sign he is there, maybe not to call us home but
To help us understand, he may be saying, follow me!
And I shall supply the key to the next journey forward
In your life.
So, we may have the riches, we hope to see in this life.
As we follow him.
But, somehow, we must know in our heart and in our soul,
Exactly, what is our aim and goal?
I believe, JESUS would say: keep thine eyes on me.
And never look away, I just imagine,
HE shall allow you to understand, he will
Lead and guild, you all the way in your trials
Of life, every step of the way.
Just remember, he is always there.
Deep down in your heart, he shall lift your
Burden right from the start.
He knows the hearts which are true, he knows
The good and the bad, happy or sad.
Believe, it he knows.

Keep the faith in him, search for the good things in your life,
Because, he is the only answer to any problem,
Within our heart.
Stay close to him, he will not part, seek for him,
And await his call,
He is there to show you, his eyes.
So, you shall not fall.

"A PRAYER"

DEAR LORD, I intend to share my love with you,
Every day and every night,
Like a vapor, of water, spreading thru out the air, we breath.
I know it comes from your every lasting power.
LORD, I humbly ask you to give me the strength, to always love.
So, I may feel your blessings from above.
In my steps of my daily walk, please
Guild my feet, in the way they must go.
As I endeavor to share your precious love.
Hold my trembling hand, as I walk across
These borrowed lands.
Guild my tongue, as I talk, to tell others of your goodness.
Lead me to the way of righteous, and hold me
So, I shall not stumble or fall.
Just keep me in your precious love, inscribed in my heart,
Forever. A-MEN.

"AN ANGEL"

If an angel were to stop by and visit you today, wonder
Exactly what that angel has in mind for you to say?
And if it were to look at you, directly in your eyes,
Wonder what really? will be the big surprise.
Just wonder now, if you took a second look,
To say hello, or a gentle goodbye.
Yes, by now, you wonder why, this perfect ANGEL DID NOT PASS YOU BY.
The question is why, it came to visit you?
Just stop, and think, this may be a warning, just for you,
To continue with the good things that you may see to do.
But, when you look up once again,
You may see pairs of angels, in front of you.
At this time, just stop and touch yourself,
Just to verify it is really you.
(on the other hand)
Ask yourself, one more question?
AM I ON EARTH, OR IN HEAVEN? FLYING AROUND WITH YOU?
(THE ANGEL)

"CAPTAIN OF THE SHIP"

Asked the question? Is your ship, ready to go out to SEA?
Just remember, it is you, and not me.
Keep in mind, you are the CAPTAIN, and think of what,
Captains are engaged to do.
You are attempting to guide, your own ship, and you are alone.
So, you must focus on your task, and be the best, you can be.
Keep your eyes opened, so you are able to survive,
And stay on course in the right direction.
You are your own protection.
In my opinion, we all are captains of our ship.
We, shall encounter, many distractions, while we are captains,
But we have a job to complete, before the
Winds and the waves dive in front of you, and cloud your clear view.
Keep in mind, again it is you.
However, you must be prepared, to make a change,
So, put on your armor, to combat the dangers ahead,
And thank GOD,
For your safety, and leading you to the still waters,
Of the sea.
The winds and the waves are at GOD'S WILL,
As "told to us, HE said, PEACE BE STILL".

"CAUGHT IN THE NET"

Imagineering being caught, in a net,
Such as: a fish, for example, if you have ever been fishing,
A tiny fish trying to escape, but it is trying to make its way
Back into, the muddy waters, or maybe even the clear waters,
But it is trying to survive.
We know that part of the story.
So, the tiny fish swims back into the deep waters of blue,
That continue on and on in front of you.
You must know, we are sometime like the tiny fish,
Trying to find our way, out of the net, in which we are caught,
At that time.
It seems, sometime LIFE holds us in a net,
Until we figure a way out, we try, and try again,
And think there is no way to WIN.
Suddenly, we figure it out, the net has become so OLD,
It begins to break, yes, break into many pieces of tiny shreds,
And they finally float away, and disappear.
Now, is your moment to collect your thoughts.
You suddenly think once again,
This is your big opportunity
To release yourself.

DON'T ROCK YOUR BOAT

I shall start by sharing with you, these words,
Do not disturb the path way of your
Because it is moving right along,
Just keep it afloat.
However, watch the direction in which
It moves.
Because you are in charge,
You are the one who knows the true direction
Ahead of you, so keep it on the moving waters and

The rippling waves of time, because time has a message for you.
Please do not look back for me, you shall be fine.
In spite of all the waters sounding you,
You shall make it, just in the appointed time.
This time is meant just for you.

"FINGER PRINTS OF JESUS"

As I paint this picture, in my mind on today, I

Envision finger prints of JESUS,
And if it were of just cause,
I believe it is justified, from the HOLY SPIRIT.
Because these prints are HOLY. (in my opinion)
And they shall never fade.
Because they are indelible prints of JESUS,
Meaning forever, in my mind.
I only imagine the sweet silence of GOD'S
Quite command saying:
With these prints, they shall always stand, within my HOLY HANDS.
To share with all of my children in HEAVEN.
This thought travels within my mind, and brings chills to my body.
It reminds me of a conversation, I had with my grandson,
When, he was very young.
(it goes like this)
He says to me" grand -ma, when you get to HEAVEN,
TELL GOD, I SAID HELLO!"
I was stunned, coming from him, just a child,
I felt ecstatic in the moment, at that time.
It made me think, once more, when we strive in every way,
Maybe when the time arrives, we shall see
those FINGER PRINTS SOME DAY.

FINGER PRINTS (continued)

When I pray, I always ask GOD! To keep us in the palm of his hands.
And some day, we may be a part of

HIS FINGER PRINTS IN HEAVEN.

"GLIDE"

As my fingers, glide across the smooth paper of many colors,
It does not matter, what the age!
My fingers see every word, as they tell a story
That has never been heard!
My fingers seem to have a special talent, only,
Known by me, because they hear, understand, and even see,
The very next word called out to be!
A spectacular unknown, word to me.
Until my thoughts begin to tango and attempt to figure
It all out, then I discover everything, without any doubt,
And my mind is very clear.
The story, they may tell, shall always be remembered,
In the hearts, of others, because, in an ironic way of,
Speaking, I wish to keep others on the path of wondering,
What is next?
However, in my next words, in my next note played on my
Piano, just may bring someone to sing the next song.
A song of joy, peace, hope, and ambition, pushing
Toward the next door to be opened, for someone,
On the very next day.
We hope it's to greet the rising sun, it may be a perfect rain drop.

GLIDE (continued)

Or even a beautiful developed snowflake, that
May not land on the solid rock on which we stand.
now you see, my fingers may tell it all,
so others may not experience that tuff fall.
We all have been there, right?
I share with you; my fingers are important to you and to me.
Because, they are telling the story,
And I pray these fingers continue to GLIDE
ACROSS THE PAGES OF TIME.

"A CUP OF TEA"

Please,
Sit and have a cup of tea, with me.
It has been a very long day; I will enjoy your company.
Yes, it is so tasty, and makes me feel complete,
With a sugar cookie and a cup of tea,
Makes your visit nice and sweet.

So, please take the weight off of your trying feet.
Come into my private parlor, and have a seat.
We shall sit and actually chat for a bit.
I take it to be ok, you have no reason not to stay.
Our little visit means so much to me.
Our love and friendship shall always be,
Together, just you and just me.

"SNOW FLAKE DIAMONDS"

I see the snow flakes, gently falling down,
Landing gently on the snow-covered frozen ground.
In this moment, we, do not hear a solitary sound.
As they swiftly, cover this frozen ground.
Only imagine, if one could count them by the millions,
As they are falling down.
And forming a glistening, shiny crown.
Giving the world a chance, to see this glorious snow flake,
Not just for you and me. but
Oh! What a sight to see.
It is coming from the HEAVENS ABOVE,
Implicating, love, love, love.
In each snow flake that falls today, it is giving us a story for all.
Reminding us, of a special day,
Made for everyone to say.
Thank you, GOD! for your snow flake diamonds
Falling from: HEAVEN ON TODAY.

"THE LIGHT"

Yea, I speak to you by saying:
The light, you shall see it, you shall touch it,
And you shall feel it, as the sunlight coming from HEAVEN.
Shinning upon you, and giving you strength,
To carry on.
This light shall provide you with the warmth,
Energy, love, joy, and peace.
It shall give you comfort, it shall be a companion,
To you.
It shall brighten your days, and guild each step
You attempt to make.
This light is your life, you may share, with others.
So, find your light and let it so shine from your heart,

And create a glow, that everyone shall know.
They may even see it in the far distance.

"THE TIME IS NOW"

The time is now to make a change.
The time is now, to receive your gain.
The time is now, to come to a stop,
But after that stop, we must continue on,
No steps, back or no turning back.
Just continue on the trail ahead,
Because, if you do not, there are others, following you
On this mysterious journey.
They may or may not survive, if they aren't able to stay alive.
I say again,
The time is now! To create a new start.
Walk forward, do not give up or stop.
Be proud, be faithful, lose no time, because we are
Counting on every mind.
OUR GOD!
in HEAVEN, shall make our day, by leading US his righteous way.

"THE TRAIN"

I say to you, please catch that train, catch it because it is leaving.
Catch it! Catch it!
You haven't time to waste.
Run, run, run, yell out! Ha, wait for me!
So, you may see the beauty of the scenery as you travel.
On that train.
Yes, in my opinion, a new view in sight just for you,
Will open new ideals for you, on this journey, as you travel.
It shall also, provide you with a fresh insight
On your future.
Just view the scenery in front of you,
And the highs and lows shall become valuable to you.
And the slops are made evenly, as your travel goes.
Look at the colors of rust, green, and yellow trees.
As you feel the gentle breeze. You are FREE
To think.
The flowers growing on the edge of the lands
In fullest bloom, of delicate colors at the command of your hand.
By now, these things have caught your attention.
As you indulge in GOD'S BEAUTY,
Of the land.

THE TRAIN (continued)

Offering you a new gift into your own hands.
And into your warm HEART.
Please take time to thank that train,
For slowing down, giving you an opportunity
Of grasping a moment of time to think, what is next for you?
Believe me, YOU SHALL FIGURE IT OUT,
On your own.
When it is time to get off the train, things will not be the same.

TODAY, OUR TOPIC IS:

"TIME"

Special time for my readers:
In the beginning of time, we think of the BOOK OF" GENESIS"
Where things all started, such as
"THE HEAVENS AND EARTH WERE CREATED BY GOD."
known as six days of time,
The seventh day, as "written, "GOD RESTED".
Now, In my opinion,
TIME is at the top of any list, it should be the priority,
In our life.
And time plays an important part of our everyday life.
With that being said, time must be used with,
Wisdom, knowledge, skills and good judgement.
And of course, with good choices.
First, we must learn the following:
We, must learn to live, love, share and respect others.
Because, in the same moment, we may be wiped away
By a wave, of the unknown? As we could view the wave of an ocean,
Rising with force, up and down the ocean waters.
In a flash, they disappear, but in TIME, that wave catches our attention.
Again, TIME IS VERY IMPORTANT IN OUR LIFE.

Time (continued)

We need to take time to STOP and pay attention to ourselves
And the world around us.
For example, maybe just maybe, our dreams shall come true in TIME.
Again, in my opinion, we live on a time line.
Just take time, and imagine, in your own mind.
Where is my friend? TIME!
Once again, we need to take time to listen,
For example, back in the day, we often heard, the phase,
And I quote: "STOP, LOOK AND LISTEN, before we cross the street,
Some time, I think it would be nice to reflect on those old moments.
IF WE TAKE THE TIME.
To listen to our children, our parents, teachers, friends, and above all
"AUTHORITY"
And some of our authority begins with OUR SCRIPTURE LESSON,
Just stop, and maybe, we shall receive a true BLESSING,
JUST TAKE TIME, BEFORE IT DISAPPEARS.
Don't allow it to be too late, and you /we can't catch up.
I believe we; all have an appointed TIIME in our life.
We need to use our TIME, wisely, example:
Take time with family, visit mom and dad.
Take time with your children.
Your partner, your lover, your wife/husband, family members.

Time (continued)

Please select something, or someone.
When you have the opportunity to share TIME.
This will make LIFE a BETTER place to live,
Just apply yours,

(TIME).

"TURNING BACK, THE DAY BEFORE TODAY"

Turning back, just ask the question?
What if your choices were better, yesterday?
Today? Or tomorrow?
Now think of the challenge you may have,
Before you.
What differently? Would you change?
For example:
A smile, a grin, a tear, behavior pattern,
Your ideals about life?
All of these questions and the answers will impact
Your life.
The question, is HOW ARE YOU FEELING TODAY?
Coping with the triumphs of daily living.
What and where are your dreams?
Are they with you now? or were they with you yesterday?
Or will it be tomorrow?
Some time we, must take a survey of our own life.
We will learn a life time of information about one self.
We must have the courage, strength, and the ability
To proceed for our future.
Because, if not, life can become most difficult.

Continued:
THE DAY BEFORE TODAY

Please remember, your choice is to cultivate
Your future.
Life will be worth living.
Because, life is trial and error.
But in the end, it is worth your time.
It is your LIFE.
It was yesterday, it is today, and shall be TOMARROW.
With your own prayers.

"A BLANKET OF GREEN"

I, remember years ago, on one early SPRING day,
I was lying on a soft GREEN blanket, but in reality, it was,
Soft green grass.
As I sat there, inhaling a sweet scent of the flowers nearby,
The scent of violets, taking my breath.
As I counted them one by one,
A few of them had fallen to the ground,
Not making any obvious sound.
And as I continued looking in the outer space,
None other to take my quiet place.
However, thinking of those ole days,
Of a calm welcome, to SPRING, it was so quiet,
And peaceful in this special space, a least for me.
In the next moment, I felt the need to rest,
Then gently closing my eyes, I suddenly felt a
Gentle kiss, on my powerless lips,
And I could not resist, in this perfect moment.
However, it was not a stranger, to my surprise,
It was someone I knew and respected so,
And I did not desire for him to go.
It was my secret partner, and I must say,
He stopped by to create a special moment in my day.

A BLANKET OF GREEN (continued)

But only wishing in that private world of mine,
Only wishing, that kiss had other options not to end.
But only BECAUSE we together made an indelible
Impression upon each other, and could not end that perfect blend.
On our WEDDING DAY OF SNOW-WHITE DIAMONDS,
And accepting that special
BLANKET OF SOFT GREEN
TO COMPLETE THAT UNFORGETTIBLE SCENE.

"A BREATH OF FRESH AIR"

As you wonder in the desert land engaged in seeking
The sites, suddenly you wish to catch a breath of fresh air,
But as you continue to walk, you stop to catch your breath
For fresh air, to rejuvenate your journey, in the desert,
Providing your body and soul a new awaking.
Once again you continue your journey,
Just to clear your mind of the past, and many things
On your agenda to make it complete.
But for the present time, you must continue on your path
And enjoy the sweet scent of fresh AIR.
Given to you from a HIGHER POWER.
And that is a blessing for you on your journey.
As you continue to walk, suddenly you notice, you have become
Hungry and thirsty, however your attention is focused
On your walking and to enjoy the fresh air.
But now you are grasping for your BREATH,
You need to stop and rest, suddenly you fall asleep,
And when you awaken, you realize the air is polluted,
Causing you difficulty in breathing, so you begin to yell
For help! However, no one hears you, and you find
Your self-struggling against the wind,
And suddenly you find yourself walking slowly,

A BREATH OF AIR (continued)

And now you observed some flowers, alone the way,
And the mountains in the far distance,
And by now you are thinking, the mountains are so far away,
In the distance ahead of you. You are thinking what, shall I do?
As you continue on, you now notice a sweet
Taste of silence as never before!
A silence that appears not to be a part of REALITY,
And it causes you to think, what does this mean to me?
This experience, what message is it sharing with me?
You also notice, the longer you walk, the farther you seem
From reality, you are now beginning to realize
In your mind, the distance is moving ahead of you,
A sign of TIME MOVING AS YOU TRAVEL,
Realizing TIME does not need permission to MOVE.
It just simply MOVES!
So, you finally realized once again, the struggle of REALITY.
Now in this moment, you feel a BREATH OF FRESH AIR,
It enhances your moment of real truth in this LIFE.
Sometime the help is within our own being, and the gift coming from GOD
In our walk with him, because he is with us always,
giving us will to live. THANK "HIM."

"A PERFECT RAIN DROP"

IF I WERE A PERFECT RAIN DROP, AND HAD
THE POWER TO SAVE THE WORLD,
OH, WHAT A WONDERFUL WORLD, THIS WOULD BE.
HOLDING THIS MESSAGE WITH IN MY HEART,
AND WANTING TO SHARE WITH YOU AND ME.
A NEW AND PERFECT START.
IF I HAD THE ABILITY TO SEE INSIDE A CRYSTAL BALL,
THIS RAIN DROP WOULD OFFER SECRETS
FOR ONE AND ALL.

HAVING THE STRENGTH, TO EXPAND MY THOUGHTS,
AND TO SHARE THE GIFTS OF LARGE OR SMALL
JUST HAVING ENOUGH, FOR EVERY ONE,
I BELIEVE IN MY HEART AGAIN, LIFE SHALL LIVE
AND NEVER END,
INSIDE THIS AMAZING PERFECT RAIN DROP.

"A FROZEN WATER FALL"

STOP, I SEE A FROZEN WATER FALL, NOT A DROP OF
WATER TO FALL, NOR A DRIP OR DIP OF WATER MOVING ANY WHERE.
NO WATER EVEN TO SPARE.
NOT A SOUND OF WATER TO BE HEARD, IN THIS SILIENT
MOMENT TO BE DISTURB. SO LET IT BE, LET IT BE.
IT IS SO PEACEFULL, AND SO STILL,
PLEASE STAY QUIET,
BECAUSE THIS EXPERIENCE IS DEFINITELY REAL.
REMINDS ME OF THE OLD GOSPEL SONG,
SHARING THE WORDS OF "PEACE BE STILL".
BEING STILL, WHAT COMES TO MY MIND
IS A QUIET SOUND IN COMMAND!
TO SAY SOFTLY, IN MY EAR, JUST BE PATIENT,
A DRIP OF WATER IS VERY NEAR.
SUDDENLY, IN THE FAR DISTANCE, I HEAR,
THE FLOWING OF WATER IS COMING SOON,
AND IT SHALL BEGIN THE GREAT WATER FALL,
JUST ABOUT NOON.
IT APPEARS TO BE THE EXCELLANCE OF NATURE.

"MAGIC WINGS"

MAGIC WINGS JUST TO FLY, ABOVE AND BEYOND,
THE DISTANT BLUE SKY.
NO SLOWING DOWN NOR COMING TO A MYSTERIOUS
STOP.
JUST, FLY, FLY, FLY.
NOT FOR A SECOND OR A MINUTE TO WORRY
ABOUT YOUR TROUBLES, RIGHT NOW,
BECAUSE YOU ARE IN THE OUTER SPACE,
AND NO OTHER TO COMMAND YOUR SPECIAL PLACE.
KEEP YOUR FOCUS AS YOU FLY,
AND EXPERIENCE THE ELMENTS AND MISTERIES IN THE SKY
YOU HAVE OFTEN HEARD AND NEVER SEEN,
A PICTURE AS THIS APPEARS AS A FANTISY
OF YOUR DREAMS.
FEEL SAFE AND FREE AS YOU FLY, NOTICE THE
TYPES OF BIRDS AS THEY SWIFTLY PASS BY.
YOUR TRAIL BEING WILD AND CARE FREE,
CONTINUE YOUR JOURNEY, WITH ADVENTURE,
YET TO SEE.
BECAUSE YOU HAVE MAGIC WINGS TO FLY.

Some days I FEEL MY HEART IS TELLING ME A STORY.
IT BEGINS LIKE THIS:
IN THE MOMENT, THERE IS A SOFT VOICE SAYING TO ME,
TAKE TIME TO LOOK, YOU MAY SEE A MIRACLE

AND IT MAY BE JESUS, A SIGN FROM THE
HEAVENS JUST FOR ME.
AT CERTAIN TIMES, I FEEL HE IS UNFOLDING THE PATHWAY
FOR ME BY SPREADING HIS BLANKET OF
BEAUTY BEFORE MY EYES.
THE BEAUTY OF A RAINBOW SHARING THE RADIANT COLORS
IN THE DISTANT SKYS.
ONLY CREATED BY A POWER GREATER THAN OURS.
THIS PICTURE DISPLAYS TO ME A SIGN OF
HOPE, FAITH, AND COURAGE PROVIDING ME
WITH THE STRENGTH I NEED TO SUCCEED
TOMARROW.
AND PERHAPS HELP SOME ONE ON THEIR
JOURNEY TO FIND WHERE THEY NEED TO BE.

"STEP BY STEP"

TRY TO EXPERIENCE LIFE STEP BY STEP,
TO ENSURE A POSITIVE OUT COME,
MAYBE, YOUR DREAM, A LEGACY, OR EVEN A VICTORY,
AS YOU MAY STRIVE TO ACHIEVE YOUR GOAL,
IN OBTAINING THE FULLNESS OF LIFE.
TAKING ONE STEP AT A TIME OPENS
OPPERTUNITIES FOR US TO SLOW OUR PACE,
AND COMPLETE THE RACE MEANT FOR US.
EVERY ONE HAS A RACE TO RUN,
IT IS UP TO EACH PERSON TO RUN, RUN, RUN.
HOW EVER, BE AWARE OF THINGS AROUND YOU,
INCLUDING THE UPS AND DOWNS, YOU
MAY EXPERIENCE.
TRY TO ENJOY YOUR STEPS, REMEMBER THEY ARE YOUR STEPS.

A SHORT STORY

"A MOMEMT OF FRIGHT"

This story begins like this,
Once there was a little girl, at the tender age of 7 years old.
I remember a terrible car accident, the screeching of tires
And crashing of glass, and all of a sudden,
An incredible haut, like stop!
The noise was loud and clear,
Cars had stopped and suddenly RED LIGHTS APPEARED.
"I was told"
Suddenly, a siren as in the tune, to the sound of an
Unpleasant song, as what in the world is wrong?
By this time a hospital trip was in to play,
And by now people not knowing just what to say?
In a few days, I was told, a young child,
Had been hit by more than one car.
This child was hit they, said" by oncoming cars,"
This young child was unconscious for days,
And then she finally awakens, and was lost for words to say.
A few more days had gone by, and this little child,
Wondered? Where was I.
When the truth was finally shared,

a moment of fright (continued)

This little girl was blessed to be living.
Yet, wondering what had happened to her,
On that cold, cold, day, with snow on the ground,
No grass to be found.
Finally, she was told, the entire story of that tragic day.
After months of lying in that little bed, in a Hugh
HOSPITAL the family said.
To this little girl, it appeared, like a city all of its own.
The little girl and the walls alone.
However, every one, dressed in white,
She thought, what an unusually site!
It appeared, scary to her in the middle of
The silent night.
By now, a few more months has passed by,
And the sound of a small little cry was passing bye.
A LITTLE BIRD
Was gently heard.
Finally, the entire story was told, about the details,
of the events, that lasted, for months on end.
This little girl, was unable to walk,
And the choice was a wheel chair, with cast on her legs half way.
She was able to go from place to place, and
maintain school assignments too.

a moment of fright (continued)

However, at a much faster pace, she worked ahead on assignments.
With the assist of her DAD, whom she loved so much,
She remembered his loving and tender touch.
She was in this wheel chair for a long time,
But her dad was there from day to day,
To take her out to play, only in her wheel chair,
She had her toys.
Which brought her lots of joy?
She also remembers going to CHURCH on SUNDAY,
Looking forward to that Monday.
Yet later in those months to come,
She remembered, what happen on that day,
Many years later she did recall, she had suddenly
Experienced a terrible fall,
Crossing a Hugh intersection, on her way to school.
But suddenly she on that day did not make it
Across the street all the way.
And woke up in a HOSPITAL,
With different people to meet. (At that time.)
This story happened many years ago,
And now you, my readers must know!
The little girl is now sharing with you, her story in her POETRY.

"EXERCISE ON BRAIN FOCUS"

7A WAY OUT

Sometime people look for a way out!

The question is: out of what??

Trouble
Marriage
Bondage
Abuse
Fear
Relation ships
Darkness
Storms
Weather (rain, snow, sun, hurricanes, tornados, floods, winds) to name a few.
Shame
Business matters
Family concerns
Education, such as school, college,
Jobs, and promotions.
Out of the spot light, as in entertainment world.
Violence
Wealth may create concerns of finding a way out?

Find a way out (continued)

Health concerns

War

FINANCE CONCERNS

No matter what, you may think of (your way out, even trouble times,
There is always hope in any situation:
(As in PSALM 130: 2, 3, 4, 5, 6.)
Ask the lord to hear your voice:" let thine ears be attentive to
The voice of my supplications." KJV
Just remember to keep the faith and hope and
Pray for strength that will help you make good decisions.
IN FINDING YOUR WAY OUT.

"BEAUTY AND DESTRUCTION"

The rippling of the waters, and the roaring of the seas, took so
Many FAMILIES, yet stretched out a wave to save me.
Yet we may wonder why? This act of nature appeared,
Oh so great! With power, it is not for us to know or even undertake.
It all just happened, in the blink of an eye,
Underneath a blanket, of the deep blue sky.
Many people lost their family and their beautiful homes
Yet for us, it is a question? Of an unknown.
Some people waited for prayers and miracles to fall
From our beautiful HEAVENS above.
The beauty of the islands was swept away so fast,
It was impossible for everything to last.
There was not time for anyone to complete any task.
It is not for us to know or comprehend why?
This beauty was destroyed, and brought to an END.
This beauty served its time on EARTH, for us all to enjoy,
Every man, woman, girl and boy.
But how has destruction moved its powerful hand?
For something else to replace it on this promise land.
Some eyes that shared this BEAUTY are not here any more
To roam, only to leave the memory of an everlasting home.

BEAUTY AND DESTRUCTION (continued)

The destruction of the lands, our WORLD shall never forget,
But only GOD in HEAVEN has the power to grant,
Us a second chance, to live for the love ones,
Gone on ahead, we must prove our love for others,
As we continue to share the gift of love, hope, and prosperity
In our life time.

"TIME"

Time is looking at us; however, we hope life shall change
Our way of thinking and create a new second, minute
And new hour, most of all a new day.
We need to pray for a new way to lead, guild and
Direction for the next call in our situations.
Life is just asking for us to be kind, gentle, and to love
One another.
So when we hear the trumpet sound, we shall not
Fret or frown. We shall hear the call not to stumble or fall.
Because Time is catching up with us.
we may wonder is time winding up or down
one thing for sure it is here, close and dear to us.
Let us hold on to the line, because our hope is
In time.

"SHUT IN"

TODAY EVERYONE IS SHUT IN OR OUT OR DOWN
AND OUR FACE HAS SUCH A FROWN.
WE WONDER WHY THIS COULD BE, YET WE PLAINLY SEE,
OUR PROBLEMS EVERYWHERE.
WE, THAT HAVE THE STRENGTH TO ENDURE
MUST WAIT TO TAKE THAT TOUR.
THINGS WE MAY NOT AGREE OR PLAINLY SEE
IN THE END PLEASE LET US AGREE.
LIFE IS ALLOWING US A SECOND CHANCE.

"A new hour"

"EMPTY SHELVES"

EMPTY SHELVES IN FRONT OF ME
AS I WALK EACH ILE SO CAREFULLY,
WITH MY HEAD HELD SO HIGH, I PEEK THRU
THE WINDOWS AND SEE A BLUE SKY.
AS I LOOK THOSE SKYS TELL ME TO KEEP THE HOPE
AND THE FAITH, OUR GOD SHALL PROVIDE HIS
AMAZING GRACE.
THRU THESE STRUGGLES, OF PAIN AND CHILLS,
YET WE ARE ABLE TO WALK SIDE BY SIDE
AND SHARE THE PROMISE GOD SHALL PROVIDE.
IN THESE CRISIS THAT WE SHARE JUST KEEP THE FAITH
OUR BURDENS HE WILL SHARE.
IN THE END, WE SHALL WIN THE VICTORY AND
SOON THOSE EMPTY SHEVLES SHALL BE
FULL ONCE MORE TO TELL THE STORY
WE MUST ADORE.
OF JOY, PEACE, HAPPNIESS, AND MOST OF ALL
LOVE OF WHICH EVERY ONE MAY ENJOY

'BOOKS'

STACKING BOOKS

Stacking books, a different. Style, when someone,
Is sitting or walking in the isles.
Share your thoughts, with others you know,
Then you find which direction, they must go?
Stack them up, or stack them down,
Stack them level to the ground!
I DO NOT CARE, JUST STACK THEM,
AND COMPLETE THE TASK,
THANK YOU, NOW YOU MAY GO HOME AT LAST.
I DO APPRECIATE YOU. (smiles).

"BUILD YOUR OWN" BOOK # 5
WE, ARE FIND TO BUILD OUR (OWN)
WITH OUR OWN IDEALS, AMBITIONS, DESIRES,
AND DREAMS, AND TO ADD A LITTLE BIT OF HOPE,
OF COURSE, GIVES US THE SPICE WE NEED
TO POSSIBLY ENTER The DOOR TO SUCCESS.
WHEN WE BUILD OUR OWN, PERHAPS,
THIS SHALL SET THE TONE TO SUCCEED.
AND JUST MAYBE WE, SHALL BE AMONG
THE BEST OF THE BEST.
WE ALL AS A PEOPLE WANT THE BEST,
AND SOME TIME THERE IS A PRICE TO PAY,
BUT IN THE END THE REWARD IS WORTH
OUR EFFORTS.
STOP AND THINK ABOUT IT, WE –R–
UNABLE TO CREATE A WORLD IN 7 DAYS,
YET, WE MAY WORK A LIFE TIME,
IN ATTEMPT, TO PERFORM OUR BEST,
BECAUSE OUR INTENTIONS ARE GOOD.
AFTER ALL, THE KEY IS: your life, my life, and
Our life. (right)?
Life in general is waiting on our call, it is our own
Determination, not to fail or fall.
Because our own efforts make the difference.

Build your own, continued

Some time it takes a life time, to unfold the core,
For us to understand much more about our own.
It is only what we build for the end product.
(A HAPPY SUCCESSFUL LIFE)

"A LONG DAY"

MY FRIENDS, WAKE UP! IT'S TIME TO GET UP
AND ENGAGE IN THE EVENTS OF TODAY.
SUCH AS THE ATTEMPT TO START THINGS
MOVING YOUR WAY.
FIRST OF ALL, ALLOW YOUR FEET TO HIT THE FLOOR,
AND GET YOUR COFFEE CUP FOR MORE,
REMEMBER, OTHERS HAVE NOTHING,
THEY MAY HAVE BEEN CRYING ALL NIGHT,
WHILE YOU WERE ALSLEEP IN YOUR BED
TURNING FROM LEFT TO RIGHT.
OTHERS ARE SIMPLY TRYING TO GET IT RIGHT.
NOTHING LIKE A LITTLE HUMOR IN ONE'S LIFE
BEGINNING A LONG DAY.
(TO MY READERS, HAVE A SPECIAL DAY).

"A MESSAGE IN A DREAM"

A MESSAGE EMBRACED IN A DREAM, HAVE
YOU EVER GIVEN IT ANY THOUGHT?

IT IS STORED IN THE SAFETY ZONE, BECAUSE
IT IS MAYBE A SECRET ALL OF YOUR OWN.
HOWEVER, THE MESSAGE IS TO YOU AND YOU ALONE.
MAY BE A PATH IN LIFE NOT YET TAKEN,
BUT A DREAM ALWAYS IN THE MAKING.
NEW THINGS, NEW HOPES, NEW DESIRES,
MAYBE SOMEONE YOU JUST ADMIRE,
JUST STOP FOR A MOMENT, AND PUT INTO VISION,
LIFE JUST MAY BE, A DREAM WE ARE JUST LIVING.
FROM ONE DAY TO THE NEXT.
ON THE OTHER HAND, PLEASE REMEMBER,
A DREAM IS A DREAM, UNTIL YOU MAKE IT COME TRUE.

"A FRIEND"

QUESTIONS:
WHAT IS A FRIEND?

A PERSON WHOM SMILES WITH YOU.
A PERSON WHOM ENCOURAGES YOU AND YOUR EFFORTS.
A PERSON WHOM PRAYS WITH YOU AND FOR YOU.
A PERSON WHOM TAKES YOU (IN) WHEN TIMES ARE TUFF,
AND OFFERS THEIR LOVE, TO YOU SO MUCH.
A PERSON WHOM WILL BUILD YOU UP,
AND THEN TAKE THE BLOCKS FROM YOU.
A PERSON WHOM OFFERS A MEAL AND PROVIDES YOU WITH
A BED TO STAY.
A PERSON TO HOLD YOUR HAND, AND SUPPORT YOU TO STAND.
UNTIL THE END, ALWAYS THERE AND WILLING TO SHARE.
ALL OF THESE THINGS, MAY BE YOUR FRIEND,
JUST COUNT YOUR BLESSINGS UNTIL THE END.
YOU SHALL KNOW YOU ALWAYS HAVE
A FRIEND IN (JESUS).

"BUILD YOUR OWN"

WE, ARE FIND TO BUILD OUR (OWN)
WITH OUR OWN IDEALS, AMBITIONS, DESIRES,
AND DREAMS, AND TO ADD A LITTLE BIT OF HOPE,
OF COURSE, GIVES US THE SPICE WE NEED
TO POSSIBLY ENTER TO DOOR TO SUCCESS.
WHEN WE BUILD OUR OWN, PERHAPS,
THIS SHALL SET THE TONE TO SUCCEED.
AND JUST MAYBE WE, SHALL BE AMONG
THE BEST OF THE BEST.
WE ALL AS A PEOPLE WANT THE BEST,
AND SOME TIME THERE IS A PRICE TO PAY,
BUT IN THE END THE REWARD IS WORTH
OUR EFFORTS.
STOP AND THINK ABOUT IT, WE –R–
UNABLE TO CREATE A WORLD IN 7 DAYS,
YET, WE MAY WORK A LIFE TIME,
IN ATTEMPT, TO PERFORM OUR BEST,
BECAUSE OUR INTENTIONS ARE GOOD.
AFTER ALL, THE KEY IS: your life, my life, and
Our life. (right)?
Life in general is waiting on our call, it is our own
Determination, not to fail or fall.
Because our own efforts make the difference.

Build your own, continued

Some time it takes a life time, to unfold the core,
For us to understand much more about our own.
It is only what we build for the end product.
(A HAPPY SUCCESSFUL LIFE)

"A LONG DAY"

MY FRIENDS, WAKE UP! IT'S TIME TO GET UP
AND ENGAGE IN THE EVENTS OF TODAY.
SUCH AS THE ATTEMPT TO START THINGS
MOVING YOUR WAY.
FIRST OF ALL, ALLOW YOUR FEET TO HIT THE FLOOR,
AND GET YOUR COFFEE CUP FOR MORE,
REMEMBER, OTHERS HAVE NOTHING,
THEY MAY HAVE BEEN CRYING ALL NIGHT,
WHILE YOU WERE ALSLEEP IN YOUR BED
TURNING FROM LEFT TO RIGHT.
OTHERS ARE SIMPLY TRYING TO GET IT RIGHT.
NOTHING LIKE A LITTLE HUMOR IN ONE'S LIFE
BEGINNING A LONG DAY.
(TO MY READERS, HAVE A SPECIAL DAY).

"A MESSAGE IN A DREAM"

A MESSAGE EMBRACED IN A DREAM, HAVE
YOU EVER GIVEN IT ANY THOUGHT?

IT IS STORED IN THE SAFETY ZONE, BECAUSE
IT IS MAYBE A SECRET ALL OF YOUR OWN.
HOWEVER, THE MESSAGE IS TO YOU AND YOU ALONE.
MAY BE A PATH IN LIFE NOT YET TAKEN,
BUT A DREAM ALWAYS IN THE MAKING.
NEW THINGS, NEW HOPES, NEW DESIRES,
MAYBE SOMEONE YOU JUST ADMIRE,
JUST STOP FOR A MOMENT, AND PUT INTO VISION,
LIFE JUST MAY BE, A DREAM WE ARE JUST LIVING.
FROM ONE DAY TO THE NEXT.
ON THE OTHER HAND, PLEASE REMEMBER,
A DREAM IS A DREAM, UNTIL YOU MAKE IT COME TRUE.

"A FRIEND"

QUESTIONS:
WHAT IS A FRIEND?

A PERSON WHOM SMILES WITH YOU.
A PERSON WHOM ENCOURAGES YOU AND YOUR EFFORTS.
A PERSON WHOM PRAYS WITH YOU AND FOR YOU.
A PERSON WHOM TAKES YOU (IN) WHEN TIMES ARE TUFF,
AND OFFERS THEIR LOVE, TO YOU SO MUCH.
A PERSON WHOM WILL BUILD YOU UP,
AND THEN TAKE THE BLOCKS FROM YOU.
A PERSON WHOM OFFERS A MEAL AND PROVIDES YOU WITH
A BED TO STAY.
A PERSON TO HOLD YOUR HAND, AND SUPPORT YOU TO STAND.
UNTIL THE END, ALWAYS THERE AND WILLING TO SHARE.
ALL OF THESE THINGS, MAY BE YOUR FRIEND,
JUST COUNT YOUR BLESSINGS UNTIL THE END.
YOU SHALL KNOW YOU ALWAYS HAVE
A FRIEND IN (JESUS).

"EXTRAORDINARY DAY"

SHARING WITH YOU AN EXTRADINARY DAY.
WHILE DRIVING IN MY CAR ON A BRIGHT AND SUNNY DAY,
I WAS KIND OF GAZING INTO THE OPEN BLUE SKY, IN AZ. AREA.
AND ALSO KEEPING MY FOCUS ON THE ROAD WAY.
SOME HOW I TEND TO LOOK UPWARD ON A CLEAR DAY.
I LOVE THE BLUE PURE SKYS.
IN THE DISTANT SKY WAYS, I SAW TWO JET AIRPLANES,
THESE PLANES WERE FLYING AND MAKING A CRISS CROSS PATTERN,
IN THE SKY WAYS, TO MY SURPRISE,
I TOOK TIME TO STOP MY CAR, AND TAKE NOTE
OF THE TWO PLANES, AND THEIR INTERSECTING PATH.
OF COURSE, CREATING A CROSS AFFECT IN THE
SKY.
YES, A PERFECT PATTERN OF A (CROSS). (+)
I DID NOT FEEL LOST, BUT AMAZED AT THE EXPERIENCE
I HAD WITNESS, IN THE MOMENT.
IN MY MIND, AT THE TIME, MY BODY FELT HELPLESS.
THIS EXPERIENCE, BROUGHT TO MY ATTENTION,
A WHAT IF QUEESTION? SUCH AS,
THE CROSS OF JESUS IN THE SKY WAYS OF HEAVEN.
I FELT COURAGE, EXCITEMENT, FORGIVENESS,
AND MOST OF ALL LOVE.

(CONTINUED)

I FELT BLESSED HAVING SEEN THIS EXPERIENCE.
I FELT A DIVINE SUPERNATURAL POWER, IN THE MOMENT.
I MAINTAIN HOPE AND FAITH, IN MY HEART
FOR MYSELF AND OTHERS ON THIS PLANET,
AND THE WORLD, WE LIVE IN.
THE PLANES, OF COURSE, QUICKLY DISAPPEARED
AND CONTINUED ON THEIR DESTINATION.
HOW EVER, I SHARE MY STORY WITH YOU,
MY FAITHFULL READERS, MAYBE THIS WILL,
GIVE YOU TIME TO THINK, AND ASK THE QUESTION?
(WHAT IF)? THIS WERE THE HIGHER POWER,
ALLOWING US, A SECOND CHANCE.

EDNA HARDAMAN, (AUTHOR)

"DON'T BACK DOWN OR WALK AWAY"

DON'T BACK DOWN, OR WALK AWAY WHEN TIMES SEEM
TUFF, BECAUSE LIFE ALONE IS (DEFINITELY) TUFF.
SO, WITH THAT BEING SAID, LET US MOVE ON,
ONE, MUST KEEP YOURSELF TOGETHER IN OUR TIME,
OF CONFUSION, MEANING THE LACK OF UNDERSTANDING,
AND OR UNCERTAINTY.
WE HAVE TIRED BODIES, UNPLEASANT
NEWS, UNEXPECTED NEWS, (ETC.)
SO, WE MUST ENTERTAIN OUR MIND, GO ALONE AND SING YOUR
SONG.
JUST KEEP THE FAITH AND KEEP IN STEP,
DO NOT FALL BEHIND, KEEP IN TIME WITH THE MUSIC,
A YOUNG MAN TOLD ME ONCE, "MUSIC IS FOOD FOR THE SOUL"
REMEMBER LIFE MUST GO ON, IN SPITE OF OUR
DIFFICULT TIMES, WE MUST LIVE FOR THE LIVING.

"CHRISTMAS IN A BOX"

MERRY CHRISTMAS TO YOU, I AM MISSING YOU EVER SO MUCH,
A MILLION LITTLE ITEMS I, HAVE PLACED IN YOUR BOX,
EVEN A LITTLE PAIR OF SPECIAL SOCKS,
I WANT TO BRING JOY, AND SMILES SO BRRIGHT,
SO PLEASE OPEN YOUR BOX ON CHRISTMAS EVE NIGHT.
I PACKED THEM SO CAREFULLY, ONE BY ONE,
SOME TIME SITTING DOWN AND SOME TIME ON THE RUN.
BUT THEY WERE PLACED IN YOUR BOX WITH TENDER LOVING
CARE, WISHING AND HOPING I COULD BE THERE.
HOW EVER OUR LOVE SHALL MEET, WHEN YOU OPEN
YOUR BOX AND TAKE A PEEK.
YOU WILL BE HAPPY WITH THE CHRISTMAS TREETS,
WITH SO MANY GOOD THINGS TO EAT.
CHRISTMAS SHALL BE HERE IN A FEW DAYS,
IT BRINGS JOY AND PEACE IN NUMEROUS WAYS.
COOKIES, CANDY AND POP CORN TOO, WERE PACKED SO GENTLY,
JUST FOR YOU.
THIS PAGE DEDICATED TO TWO SONS
FROM A LOVING (MOM).

"WATERS EDGE"

NOTICE THE WATERS EDGE, FOR EXAMPLE, IT SLOWLY MOVES
AS IT RISES OR DESCENDS.
CONSTANTLY, MOVING ALL ABOUT HEARING
THE WATERS, MOVE IN AND OUT,
SOME TIME PEOPLE ARE SIMULAR TO THE WATERS EDGE
AS DESCRIBED ABOVE,
INCLUDEING THE RELEVANT QUALITIES
AND THE EVENTS TAKING PLACE
AT THE TIME.
JUST TAKE TIME TO OBSERVE ANY WATERS EDGE,
SOME TIME GIVING AND SOME TIME BEING SILENT, AS IN(STILL).
SOME TIME WATER IS DEVASTATEING TO US,
BECAUSE THE NATURE OF WATER HAS ITS OWN
CHARACTERISTICS SERVING TO IDENTIFY,
MEANING PEOPLE AS WELL,
JUST BE AWARE OF THE POWERFUL STRENGTH OF
THE WATERS EDGE.

"DO NOT SUFFER THY PAIN"

DO NOT SUFFER YOUR PAIN
INVOLVE YOUR HEART, SOUL, AND MIND INTO AN UNTRAVELED LANE
IN LIFE.
TAKE A STROLL WITH YOUR SOUL, AND INVITE A MOMENT OF
MEDITATION AND CONVERSATION WITH SELF AND SOUL.
LEAD YOUR HEART INTO A NEW START OF WALKING FORWARD.
WHILE CONTINUING YOUR JOURNEY,
ALLOWING YOUR MIND, A CHOICE TO EMBRANCE, AND
ENHANCE YOUR THOUGHT PROCESS AND TO CONNECT
WITH IN YOUR SOUL.
IT IS POSSIBLE A NEW AND AMAZING EXPERIENCE
SHALL TAKE PLACE, INCLUDING A NEW PERCEPTION
OF YOUR OWN OUT LOOK ON YOUR LIFE.
MAKE AN EFFORT TO LIVE ABOVE YOUR LEVEL OF PAIN,
OBVIOUSLY, YOU SHALL OVER COME YOUR
SUFFERING OF PAIN IN TIME.
(IN MY OPINION), DO NOT SUFFER YOUR PAIN NEEDLESSLY.

"DON'T BACK DOWN OR WALK AWAY"

DON'T BACK DOWN, OR WALK AWAY WHEN TIMES SEEM
TUFF, BECAUSE LIFE ALONE IS (DEFINITELY) TUFF.
SO, WITH THAT BEING SAID, LET US MOVE ON,
ONE, MUST KEEP YOURSELF TOGETHER IN OUR TIME,
OF CONFUSION, MEANING THE LACK OF UNDERSTANDING,
AND OR UNCERTAINTY.
WE HAVE TIRED BODIES, UNPLEASANT
NEWS, UNEXPECTED NEWS, (ETC.)
SO, WE MUST ENTERTAIN OUR MIND, GO ALONE AND SING YOUR
SONG.
JUST KEEP THE FAITH AND KEEP IN STEP,
DO NOT FALL BEHIND, KEEP IN TIME WITH THE MUSIC,
A YOUNG MAN TOLD ME ONCE, "MUSIC IS FOOD FOR THE SOUL"
REMEMBER LIFE MUST GO ON, IN SPITE OF OUR
DIFFICULT TIMES, WE MUST LIVE FOR THE LIVING.

"DO NOT SUFFER THY PAIN"

DO NOT SUFFER YOUR PAIN
INVOLVE YOUR HEART, SOUL, AND MIND INTO AN UNTRAVELED LANE
IN LIFE.
TAKE A STROLL WITH YOUR SOUL, AND INVITE A MOMENT OF
MEDITATION AND CONVERSATION WITH SELF AND SOUL.
LEAD YOUR HEART INTO A NEW START OF WALKING FORWARD.
WHILE CONTINUING YOUR JOURNEY,
ALLOWING YOUR MIND, A CHOICE TO EMBRANCE, AND
ENHANCE YOUR THOUGHT PROCESS AND TO CONNECT
WITH IN YOUR SOUL.
IT IS POSSIBLE A NEW AND AMAZING EXPERIENCE
SHALL TAKE PLACE, INCLUDING A NEW PERCEPTION
OF YOUR OWN OUT LOOK ON YOUR LIFE.
MAKE AN EFFORT TO LIVE ABOVE YOUR LEVEL OF PAIN,
OBVIOUSLY, YOU SHALL OVER COME YOUR
SUFFERING OF PAIN IN TIME.
(IN MY OPINION), DO NOT SUFFER YOUR PAIN NEEDLESSLY.

"DON'T STOP PRAYING"

Knowing when life is surviving well, in that moment,
Don't stop praying.
It is a perfected test, for you to perform your very best.
And in times like these, don't stop praying.
Keep a smile on your face, and with GOD'S AMAZING GRACE,
Don't stop praying.
Wave to others as they attempt to take their place,
Pray for them, with GOD'S Amazing Grace.
Some may be walking on the streets, as you continue on, you
Shall greet new faces you have never seen, they also need
Your care and time to share.
Just the words, so soft, and sweet, shall be the key to
Open that unseen door for that lonely one on the street.
Don't stop praying.
When the light goes on or off, may be a sign for a new start.
Keep prayer, always on your mind,
IN TIMES LIKE THESE.
DON'T STOP PRAYING.

"FOLLOW THE STREAM"

To my readers:

As your thoughts wonder from day to day,
In an attempt to discover your true adventures in life.
Let's start by saying, you are sorting out your thoughts, trying to make
Good decisions, however you may need some assistance.
To help you prioritize your thinking process,
Stop, in my opinion your help is coming from a
Nearby stream, and you must follow it,
After you find it.
So, as you take step by step, and put one
Foot in front of the other as you walk, soon to discover,
A stream, you shall hear a stream of water, flowing
Gently and evenly, and softly in front of you.
Finally, this stream will provide you
With a feeling of solitude.
And it shall provoke your own emotions with in
Your soul.
Just follow this stream!
It may lead you across the world and back again.
But this stream may be your answer.

FOLLOW THE STREAM:

However, the outcome you shall win,
The release of discomfort in your heart.
Finally, you shall discover

You will feel free and full of love in your heart.
After collecting your thoughts,
a sigh of relief steps in, and your body begins
to tremble, in its entirety, as a streak of lightning,
flashing before your eyes.
A soft voice is saying to you, do not be afraid,
I am with you.
This is your moment, and this is your stream,
Just follow it, it will remain with you, as a
Crutch helping an injured person,
For support.

You shall not fall.
This stream becomes your own mentor.
You shall hear its continuous flow,
As you continue to go.
I just imagine, you shall find your answers,

FOLLOW THE STREAM

To your unique situation, as you follow your stream.

Do not allow it to go.

"GRAZE INTO THE WESTERN SKY"

As I sit and gaze into the beautiful WESTERN
SKYS, in the (ARIZONA AREA)
I clearly see the breath-taking experience of the flaming colors,
Displayed before my eyes, in these beautiful western skies.
As the colors appear to streak across the HEAVENLY blue sky.
In my opinion, a story is being shared. Each and every day,
In a unique way.
As they lower and finally fade away.
To me this story is secretly stored for the next,
On coming day.
A story of PEACE, CONTENT, AND SERENITY, given by
the FATHER, we hope to see in the HEAVENS
Of real peace and love.
A place where these beautiful radiant colors
Shall be ours to view and love each and every day,
And never fade away.
There shall be no storm clouds to obscure the real scene
Of beauty, placed in our possession to have and hold,
For our daily DREAM.
This is such a beautiful picture hanging in the sky.
Our FATHER GOD is sharing this special view
For all to see.

GAZE (continued)

Showing his GRACE, MERCY, and LOVE.
Coming from his untouchable HEAVENS ABOVE.
In my opinion, maybe we are not able to understand why?
GOD dips his paint brush on the HEAVENS,
so, we are able to comprehend, these mysterious skies.
However, when looking up, we see changes every second
Of the day, in some form and spectacular way.
TO MY READERS:
Just take a moment, to imagine the colors of a rain bow,
In your mind, but in a flash, they are left behind.
The clouds of numerous colors at that time.
This is a story of colors, from these skies.
And they may affect our daily lives, when we
Look up into these skies.
However, we shall find the beauty of GOD'S amazing design.
HE HAS MADE BY GRACE, POWER, AND HIS UNCONDITIONAL
LOVE, SHINING DOWN FROM ABOVE.
Remember to gaze, every now and then.
"MY FRIENDS."

"HEART BEAT"

Just think of the word, heartbeat, what comes to mind?
Heart beat is a delicate sound, right?
For example, the heartbeat of a new born baby,
How sweet the sound.
It has rhythm, playing round and round.
We cannot deny, I think it tells us a story,
Because, it has purpose, to share with others
Here is a quote"
Heart beat is "fruit of the womb as in PSALM 127: 3,4 (KJV)
Take note of this quote: Lo, "children are a heritage of the LORD."
A heart beat is precious to mankind,
We need to hear it and not be blind to the fact,
Of nature.
A heart beat is a blessing pouring out for us,
Each and every day, in unknown ways, to the human race.
BECAUSE GOD IS OUR AMAZING GRACE,
AT THE END OF THE DAY.
To my readers, remember the HEART BEAT
And you shall be ok.

HELPING OTHERS

LET US TAKE A SPOT CHECK TO DISCOVER,
IDEALS ON WHAT IT TAKES TO HELP OTHERS,
IN MY OPINION,
LETS, HAVE SOME FUN ON THE RUN.
INTELLECTUAL, OUR SKILLS OF INTELLIGENCE ARE TESTED
AS WE LEARN HOW TO BECOME BETTER
AND BECOME MORE EFFECTIVE
IN HELPING OTHERS.
OUR INTELLIGENCE ALSO HAS A HUGE IMPACT
ON EVERY ONE.
JUST FOR EXAMPLE, LET US USE A SAMPLE?
OUR FRIENDS, FAMILY, IN THE WORK PLACE,
AND IN EVERY DAY LIFE, SUCH AS DECISION MAKING,
RECONINIZING OUR EMOTIONS, AND MANAGING,
OUR EMOTIONS AS WELL, AGAIN LISTENING,
CARING, HELPING OTHERS
AND MOST OF ALL ACCEPTING CHANGE.
ALL OF THESE COMPOENTS MAKE UP THE NEXT FOUR WORDS:
INTELLECTUAL, EMOTIONAL, SOCIAL AND CHANGE.
NOTHING EVER STAYS THE SAME, SO IN THIS CASE
WHOM IS THERE TO BLAME?
THESE FOUR WORDS, PLAY THE ROLE, SO WE HAVE THE
ABILITY TO CREATE OUR BEST SKILLS, AND EXERCISE
OUR OWN TALENT.

HELPING OTHERS (continued)

THAT'S WHO WE ARE?
WE KNOW OUR SKILLS ARE TESTED, AS WE LEARN HOW TO
BECOME BETTER AND MORE EFFECTIVE IN HELPING OTHERS.
WE MUST LEARN HOW TO CHANGE, UNDERSTAND CHANGE,
IMPLEMENT CHANGE, SUPPORT CHANGE,
AND TO LISTEN, AND CARE ABOUT OTHERS
WHEN WE TRY TO PROVIDE HELP FOR OTHERS.

"HANGING BY A THREAD"

HELP ME, I AM HANGING BY A THREAD,
I NEED HELP, I NEED YOUR HELP!
THIS PEICE OF THREAD BECOMES MY ONLY HOPE
TO SURVIVE, BUT IT IS SO THIN, I AM AFRAID
I WILL FALL.
SO PLEASE COME TO CATCH ME BEFORE I FALL,
AND LAND ON THIS DUSTY, SANDY GROUND.
I AM NOW, SWINGING TO THE NORTH, SOUTH, EAST,
AND WEST, AND HANING ON MY VERY BEST,
I HAVE A CHOICE OF WHAT I MAY LIKE BEST,
ONLY IF YOU HELP ME FROM FALLING.
MY HANDS ARE PREPARED TO LAND INTO
YOUR ARMS FOR SAFTY.
I AM SEARCHING FOR STRENGTH TO KEEP ME
STRONG, AND THE WILL TO CONTINUE ON,
IF YOU CATCH ME AND KEEP ME SAFE
IN YOUR ARMS FOREVER.

Let's RIDE TOGETHER (BOOK #5)

LET'S RIDE TOGETHER, AS WE GO AROUND
ON THE OLD TIME MERRY- GO- ROUND.
IN TODAY 'S WORLD, IT IS KNOWN AS A(CAROUSEL).
IF YOU FEEL OUT OF PLACE, THIS EXPERIENCE SHALL BRING A
PLEASANT SMILE UPON YOUR FACE.
LISTEN TO THE MUSIC OF THE OLD TIME SONGS,
GIVES YOU A FEELING OF DOING NO WRONG,
THROW YOUR HEAD BACK AND TAKE SOME TIME,
HOLD YOUR BREATH AND COUNT TO NINE.
AGAIN, ENJOY THIS RIDE, IF YOU CAN, WITH OUT
INTERRUPTIONS CREATING DEMANDS.
FOR ONCE IN YOUR LIFE, ENJOY THE FEELING
OF FREEDOM.
SO HOLD ON TIGHT, NEVER LOOK AWAY, ENJOY YOUR SPECIAL DAY.
YOU MAY SOON DISCOVER WHY? WE SHARD THIS
MOMENT (TOGETHER)

"LIVE TODAY"

HI TO EVERY ONE ON TODAY,
OF COURSE, TODAY IS A NEW DAY, AND A NEW WAY
IN OUR THINKING.
IN THESE TIMES OF GLOBLE CRISIS,
TRY TO COMFORT SOME ONE AROUND YOU,
IT MAY BE FAMILY OR FRIENDS, OR A STRANGER
THINK OF KEEPING THEM SAFE AND OUT OF DANGER.
TIME IS SHARD WITH ALL OF US,
DO NOT FRET OR GIVE A FUSS.
IT DOES NOT PAY AT THE END OF OUR DAY.
TIME HAS GIVEN US AN OPPORTUNITY,
TO JUST OBEY, OUR GOOD THOUGHTS,
IN LIVING TODAY.

"LIFE LONG TEACHER"

Life is a teacher, the question is, how do we learn?
And what do we learn?
Life is a teacher for us every day.
Learning something new on our way.
Just looking back, what is in view?
What have we learned, and how may we share,
For example, today's world is such a rapid pace,
We must pick and choose our options to display, to our family
And friends each and every day.
Not a moment pass by, we know the reason why,
Because, of our TECHNOLOGY AGE.
Yes, we are now in the real world of technology.
Come rain or come shine.
It is plain as a dime, so get it together and refuse to whine
Life may be a risk at best these days, but that is LIFE
Teaching us at BEST.
we all know it is to grow and enhance our FUTURE.
If we wish to remain in insistence.
It is our decision to go for it, and do our utmost best at
Our goal, to see reality unfold.

"LIFE IS A TEACHER" (continued)

LIFE remains a teacher, take any one's guess,
Can anyone imagen, what may be NEXT?
(in my opinion)
Our life is in our own hands.
It is what we desire to make it.
That being said, take it, make it, or break it.
It is on YOU!

"LIVING TODAY"

WE –R- LIVING TODAY, IT IS EVIDENT IN OUR MIND.
AND QUITE OBVIOUS TOMARROW HAS NOT ARRIVED.
DAYS HAVE COME AND GONE, LEAVING THE
MEMORIES OF YESTERDAY ETCHED IN OUR HEART.
NO DOUBT, EACH DAY COMES BY TO VISIT US,
WE MUST EMBRACE AS NEVER BEFORE.
BECAUSE WE KNOW NOT WHAT? TOMORROW
MAY BRING.
PERHAPS, A LITTLE SUNSHINE, ADDING SHOWERS OF BLESSINGS
PLACED UPON OUR PEDESTAL, FOR THE DAY.
SO, DO NOT TAKE TIME TO LOOK AWAY.
ALLOW THE OPPORTUNITY, BY MAKING A GLORIOUS
DAY MEANINGFUL AND CREATE FEELINGS OF
DELIGHT WITH SPARKS OF ADMIRATION.

"ENDURE"

A PRAYER TO ENDURE
DEAR LORD I ASK YOU, TO GIVE ME A NEW BIRTH,
TO MY INNER SOUL, SO I MAY FEEL THE PRESENCE OF
YOUR HOLY PROMISE TO ENDURE,
SEEING PEOPLE COME AND WATCHING PEOPLE GO.
PLEASE PROVIDE THE STRENGTH, SO ALL SHALL KNOW.!
THE ONLY PATH YOU MAY DIRECT ME ON,
I FEEL IT IS JUST FOR ME.
LEAD ME, GUIDE, IN THIS LIFE,
AS I LIVE FROM DAY TO DAY.
I SHALL CONTINUE TO FOLLOW YOUR PRECIOUS WAY.

"COME BACK MY LOVE"

STANDING HERE ALONE, BUT ASKING YOU TO COME BACK
MY LOVE,
PLEASE COME BACK, MY EYES ARE FULL OF TEARS,
AND I AM UNABLE TO SEE CLEARLY.
I BARELY SEE YOU IN THE DISTANCE OF THE SKYS.
AS YOU CONTINUE TO GO, MY TEARS CONTINUE TO FLOW,
AS A WINDING RIVER, LEADING IN THE DISTANCE.
AND AFTER A WHILE, YOU ARE OUT OF MY SIGHT,
I CAN NOT SEE, OR HEAR ANY SIGN OF LIFE,
BUT I KNOW YOU ARE THERE, SOME WHERE, JUST OUT OF SIGHT.
YET TO RETURN TO ME WITH YOUR UNFORGETTABLE
LOVE.
COME BACK MY LOVE.

"READING"

IN MY OPINION, READING IS THE SEED, AND THE
UNDERSTANDING OF IT ALL, IT IS ESSENTIAL
AND NECESSARY IN LIFE,
AND HOW TO BECOME A SURVIVOR IN THE
WORLD WE LIVE IN.
TAKE TIME TO PLANT THE SEED IN YOUR HEART AND SOUL.
IT SHALL BECOME A PART OF THE SECRET NOT TO UNFOLD.
YOU SHALL FINALLY CHERISH IT AS PURE GOLD.
READING MAY BE THE KEY TO UNLOCK THE DOOR,
FOR MANY OTHERS, THERE IS ALWAYS MORE IN STORE.
AND
IT PROVIDES EVERY ONE A PORTION OF SUCCESS WHILE
IT ENHANCE PEOPLE A SECOND CHANCE
GIVING AN OPPORTUNITY TO SUCCEED.
SO, READ, READ, READ.
EDNA HARDAMAN, AUTHOR

"LOVING THE CHRISTMAS HOLIDAY"

Making a holiday special, how shall it begin, maybe
With your lover, when he or she walk into the room,
Filled with silence, no one there, but the two of you,
When you both smiles, and together you share that smile,
the two of you suddenly dissolve into one.
You are unable to blink, or even think, exactly what may be next?
You both are thinking, but keeping your silence to yourself.
By now, you may have a desire to make a step,
but you are unable to move
Because, you feel as if your entire body is
Stiff and unable to move, so your eyes are speaking for you.
They are dancing and moving about,
Because, you are unable to make a step toward the other person.
Needless to say, you are so handsome, and she is so beautiful.
You both are afraid of WHAT?
Of course, you do not know? because you cannot think of anything to say,
At this point, TIME is wasting away, and your thoughts, are yet silent,
As the MID NIGHT MOON!
At this point, both of you only share your looks with each other.
However, you both are now captivated, by your interest and charm.
Your emotions appear to be running away,
Now, if possible, put into your own words:
What selection of words, might be chosen?

To make a first step, toward your feelings for each other,
???
On this SPECIAL HOLIDAY,
IT IS EASY, JUST TO SAY
I LOVE YOU.

"A FROZEN WATER FALL"

STOP, I SEE A FROZEN WATER FALL, NOT A DROP OF
WATER TO FALL, NOR A DRIP OR DIP OF WATER MOVING ANY WHERE.
NO WATER EVEN TO SPARE.
NOT A SOUND OF WATER TO BE HEARD, IN THIS SILIENT
MOMENT TO BE DISTURB. SO LET IT BE, LET IT BE.
IT IS SO PEACEFULL, AND SO STILL,
PLEASE STAY QUIET,
BECAUSE THIS EXPERIENCE IS DEFINITELY REAL.
REMINDS ME OF THE OLD GOSPEL SONG,
SHARING THE WORDS OF "PEACE BE STILL".
BEING STILL, WHAT COMES TO MY MIND
IS A QUIET SOUND IN COMMAND!
TO SAY SOFTLY, IN MY EAR, JUST BE PATIENT,
A DRIP OF WATER IS VERY NEAR.
SUDDENLY, IN THE FAR DISTANCE, I HEAR,
THE FLOWING OF WATER IS COMING SOON,
AND IT SHALL BEGIN THE GREAT WATER FALL,
JUST ABOUT NOON.
IT APPEARS TO BE THE EXCELLANCE OF NATURE.

"MAKE TIME TO BALANCE"

TODAY IS A NEW DAY, LET US TALK ABOUT THE
WORD: BALANCE AND TIME.
AND MAYBE HOW TO MAKE IT WORK FOR US,
WHILE WE, MAY BE SITTING ON THE BUS, GOING
TO WORK, SCHOOL OR PLAY. KEEP IN YOUR MIND,
IT IS A NEW AND EXCITING DAY.
WE HAVE HEARD OF THESE TERMS, SUCH AS UPRIGHT,
STEADY, EQUILBRIUM, AND SO ON. (ETC.)
REFERING TO THE WORD BALANCE PER (WEBSTER).
HOW EVER IN THE REAL WORLD, AND IN OUR DAILY LIVES?
IT APPEARS TO BE A CONCERN, AS TO HOW?
WE SUCCEED TO MAKE IT WORK,
FOR A MOMENT, THINK ON FAMILY, HUSBAND, KIDS, JOBS,
AND OTHER EVENTS, TAKING PLACE IN OUR LIFE.
WE ALL HAVE HEARD, THESE QUOTES AS:" NOT ENOUGH TIME,
"ALLOW ME MORE TIME TO COMPLETE THE TASK,
SOME DAY I SHALL BE FINISHED AT LAST,
I NEED MORE TIME, NOT ENOUGH HOURS IN THE DAY,
TWENTY-FOUR HOURS, WE MIGHT SAY, NOT ENOUGH TIME"
WHAT A DIFFERENCE A DAY BRINGS TO US.
WHILE WE CONTINUE ON OUR BUS.
DAY AFTER DAY, WE WANT OUR OWN WAY, TO PERFORM

BALANCE (continued)

OUR OWN TASK, IF ONLY IT SHALL LAST IN
TWENTY- FOUR LITTLE HOURS.
WE LOSE TRACK OF TIME SO QUICKLY, DUE TO THE EVENTS
TAKING PLACE AT THE TIME.
TIME IS ON THE FAST TRACK IN OUR LIFE.
TIME RUNS AND APPEARS NOT TO STOP, AT
THE END OF THE NEXT BLOCK.
YET WE RECOGNIZE THE CONCERN.
AGAIN WE ALL CONTINUE TO SAY, "WHERE DID THE TIME GO?
HOW EVER, ON THE OTHER HAND (TIME IS WITH US CONTINUOUSLY)
IT IS OUR PARTNER, I THINK IT ALLOWS US TO THINK,
PLAN, AND KEEP OUR INTEREST ALIVE.
SO THE QUESTION REMAINS: HOW DO WE DEAL WITH IT?
HOW DO WE BALANCE OUR TIME?
WE, ARE DEALING WITH TIME AND BALANCE.
AFTER TAKING TIME TO READ THIS SELECTION,
(MAYBE IN MY OWN OPINION)
YOU HAVE ACCOMPLISHED SOMETHING, (RIGHT?)
HERE ARE SOME TID BITS:
YOU DID TAKE TIME TO READ SO,
START BY APPOINTIING TIME FOR SELF,
TO ORGANIZE YOUR TIME, PRIORITIZE,
IMPORTANT THINGS, DESIGNATE TO OTHERS,
COORDINATE A LIST OF TO DO THINGS,

BALANCE (continued)

AGAIN, CHANCES OF BEATING TIME IS IMPOSSIBLE
IT IS ONE OF OUR MAIN ELEMENTS TO WORK WITH,
MANY YEARS AGO, AS OUR HISTORY TELLS US,
PEOPLE HAD TIME TO PERFORM THE TASK OF THE DAY,
SIMPLY, BECAUSE BACK IN THE DAY, PEOPLE
HAD LESS TO DEAL WITH.
SO AS THE OLD SAYING "THEY MADE DO" WITH WHAT THEY HAD.
FOR EXAMPLE, THE OLD GENERAL STORE HAD MOST EVERTHING
TO MEET THEIR NEEDS.
SO TO SUM THIS UP, GENERATIONS BEFORE US, HAD
TO BALANCE THEIR TIME ACCORDINGLY TO THE EVENTS
TAKING PLACE IN THEIR LIFE.
(AT THE TIME)
EDNA HARDAMAN, AUTHOR

"MEETING YOU AT THE BEACH"

MEETING YOU AT THE BEACH, WITH SAND BETWEEN YOUR
TOES, WE LAY HERE SO QUIETLY, BUT NO ONE REALLY KNOWS,
WE NOW SHARE A SWEET KISS WITH ADDED BLISS,
SHOWING OUR TRUE AFFECTION FOR EACH OTHER.
OUR THOUGHTS, OUR WISHES, AND OUR DREAMS COME TRUE
PLANNING ON THE NEXT IMPORTANT THINGS
TO DO.
AND TO MAKE LOVE TO EACH OTHER, OUR
FEELINGS ARE SOFT AND TENDER TO THE TOUCH.
THIS SPECIAL TIME ON THE BEACH
HAS MADE OUR LOVE RESPECTFULLY COMPLETE.
NOW WE HAVE FUTURE PLANS TO MAKE,
MOST IMPORTANTLY, FUTURE STEPS TO TAKE.
A WEDDING GOWN AND WEDDING CAKE
FOR EVERY ONE TO SHARE,
WE ARE ALMOST THERE, WITH BLESSINGS.

(MORE TO COME)

LIFE SOME TIMES, APPEARS TO US, AS A WISH NEVER
ENDING, FOR EXAMPLE: A CHILD WISHING FOR A TOY AND
NEVER RECEIVING IT, BUT THE CHILD CONTINUES
TO WISH.
WE ADULTS, ARE CHILEREN THAT HAVE NOW GROWN UP.
NO MATTER THE TASTE OF THE BITTER CUP,
EARLY ON IN OUR LIFE.
WE NOW HAVE SUNSHINE AND WE HAVE RAIN,
SO AS WE LOOK UP AND SEE THE MOVING CLOUDS,
WE NOW WISH TO SEE THE SUN, AGAIN
WISHING FOR MORE TO COME OUR WAY,
BEFORE THE END OF DAY.
WE HOPE THE RADIENT SUN RAY SHALL PROVIDE
US WITH A MONEMT OF WARMTH,
ON OUR TENDER SKIN, FIGHTING THE ELEMENTS
OF THE WINDS OF NO RETURN,
PASSING SWIFTLY BY.
AT THE END OF THE DAY, WE THINK ANOTHER DAY
HAS PAST AND GONE, AND WHAT HAVE WE
ACCOMPLISHED TO HELP SOME ONE ON THIS
PARTICULIAR DAY? RIGHT OR WRONG.

MORE TO COME (continued)

(IN MY OPINION)
TIME IS JUST LOANED TO US, AS A GIFT
HAVING NO RETURN.
BUT, OPPORTUNITY MAY COME OUR WAY ONCE AGAIN,
GIVING US A CHOICE TO MAKE.
WE, (ON THE OTHER HAND) ALWAYS ASKED FOR MORE.
UNTIL OPPORTUNITY KNOCKS ONCE MORE.
WE HOW EVER ARE AWARE OF OUR OWN
SATISFACTION AND MOST TIME ACCEPT THE OUT COME
OF THE GIVEN SIUATION.
JUST IMAGENE IF TIME WERE A SPINNING BALL,
UNRAVFULLING BEFORE OUR EYES, AS A BALL OF YARN
WOVEN IN A SPINNING WHEEL, AND MAKING NO
ATTEMPT TO STOP FOR REST.
PERHAPS SEEING LIFE AS A DELUSION,
IN OUR MIND.
FIGHTING AGAINST THE EXPERIENCE OF TIME,
AS WE KNOW IT.
WE YET WAIT FOR DREAMS TO COME TRUE
AND IT APPEARS, NOT FULL FILLING,
THE ATONEMENT OF ACTIONS.
MY GUESS MAY BE, WE ARE NEVER SATIFIED
WITH WHAT EVER COMES OUR WAY, FROM DAY TO DAY.

MORE TO COME (continued)

WE NEED TO LOVE AND CHEERISH EVERY MOMENT OF LIFE,
AS IT COMES OUR WAY.
AGAIN, WE SEE BUT DO NOT UNDERSTAND THE FULLNESS
AND RICHNESS OF OUR BEING.
WE NEED TO MAKE AN ATTEMPT
TO ACCEPT CHANGE, BECAUSE LIFE OFFERS US PURPOSE
AND WE NEED TO FIND THAT PURPOSE TO
THE FULLEST OF OUR ABILITY TO MAINTAIN
BALANCE AND SKILLS USEFULL TO OURSELVES
AND OTHERS.
(IN MY OPINION) WE MUST ACT ACCORDINGLY
(AS IN PROVERBS: 2018 NIV).

"THE LITTLE COUNTRY CHURCH"

IN THE MEADOWS OF MEMORY.
AS I REMEMBER, THIS LITTLE COUNTRY CHURCH,
BRINGING SO MUCH JOY, PEACE AND LOVE
TO EVERY ONE.
STANDING WITH OPEN DOORS AND COMFORT.
INVITING EVERY GUEST TO SIT AND HAVE A SEAT,
ALSO BRINGING SOMETHING GOOD TO EAT.
TO SAY A PRAYER WITH OUT DESPAIR,
ALWAYS SINGING, THE SONGS OF GLORY,
STANDING UP TO TELL THEIR STORY.
THEY ALWAYS, REMEMBERD THEIR PRAYER
ASKING GOD TO BLESS PEOPLE EVERY WHERE.
SOME MAY COME AND SOME MAY GO.
BUT THE LITTLE CHURCH CONTINUED TO FLOW,
WITH THAT JOY HAVING GRACE, AND YET ASKING
GOD TO BLESS THIS PLACE,
CONTINUE TO KEEP YOUR CHILDREN SAFE.
WITH THY AMAZING GRACE.
MEMORIES OF THE LITTLE CHURCH IN THE MEADOWS.
BY EDNA HARDAMAN, AUTHOR

"ROCKS BENEATH THE PINES"

AS I SAT ONE DAY LOOKING AT THE ROCKS, COVERING
THE SAND COLORED GROUND,
THESE ROCKS WERE ALL COLORS, SHAPES, AND SIZES.
I WONDERED HOW THIS EXPERIENCE COULD BE,
JUST A SPECIAL TREET TO SEE.
AS THEY LAY SO QUIETLY IN THEIR PERSPECTIVE PLACE
IT WAS AMAZING TO OBSERVE, NATURE AT ITS BEST.
SOME WERE SMALL, AND SOME WERE TALL,
TO NUMEROUS TO COUNT THEM ALL.
THESE ROCKS WERE BENEATH THE PINE
TREES STANDING TALL, ABOVE.
I COULD ONLY THINK THE SIGN OF LOVE.
THESE ROCKS TO ME, WAS A REMINDER OF THE ROCKIES
IN THE WEST, WITH NATURE'S HAND AT ITS BEST.
THESE SIMPLE ROCKS BENEATH THE PINES,
SHARING WITH ME THEIR OWN MYSTERIOUS SIGN.
YES, ROCKS BENEATH THE PINES
I JUST ASSUME, THESE ROCKS AND PINES
HAVE BEEN IN THEIR PLACE
MANY YEARS AGO.
HOW EVER THEY CONTINUE TO MAKE THEIR MARK,
AND NO ONE SHALL EVERY KNOW.
THEIR TRUE STORY OF NATURE MANY YEARS AGO.
THEY SHALL MAINTAIN THEIR POWER AND BEAUTY FOREVER.

"IN THE FALL OF THE YEAR"

LEAVES ARE TURNING UP SIDE DOWN, AND GENTLY
TOUCHING THE SOLID GROUND.
THE LEAVES OF COLORS RED BROWN AND GOLD,
THEY ARE HERE TO VISIT US FOR A WHILE.
THEY SHALL NOT VISIT US VERY LONG
BECAUSE, THEY MAY DISAPPEAR IN A FLASH,
OFF TO WONDER LAND IN A DASH.
WE JUST ASSUME THEY COME AND GO,
EVERY YEAR, AS A REMINDER, WE ALL KNOW,
FALL IS NOT HERE TO STAY, BUT ONLY TO VISIT,
FOR A WHILE.
YET IT IS NICE TO SEE, VARIOUS COLORS ON THE TREE,
THIS TIME OF YEAR.
FALL IS HERE TO SHARE AND REMIND US OF THE CHANGE
TO COME, INCLUDING THE WESTERN SETTING OF THE SUN.
FALL BRINGS US PLEASURE WITH ITS RADIENT
COLORS OF RED, YELLOW, GREEN AND BROWN,
AS THEY SILENTLY TUMMBLE TO THE GROUND.

"NEVER GIVE UP"

Never, look down, always look up, but
Never give up on your stories to be told,
Never give up on yours hopes, described, as being
Bold. (qualities and or events.)
Build on your weakness, and make your life strong,
So, when the time comes, you may sing your own song.
You may eventually gain the world into your own hands.
But it will be your own world to discover, and share
With others.
Life is similar somewhat like that dream,
But when you awaken, you discover, suddenly
Life is not what it seems.
Because life is life.
All I am saying: NEVER GIVE UP! YOU may have to sip
From that bitter cup.

"OTHER SIDE OF THE STREET"

LET US OBSERVE THE OTHER SIDE OF THE STREET
OR AT LEAST TAKE A TURN DOWN THE STREET.
YES, TWO SIDES OF THE SAME STREET,
OR THE BOULEVARD AS WELL.
THERE IS A STORY TO TELL.
ONE SIDE AS BEING DESCRIBE AS A
BETTER SIDE THAN THE OTHER, IT MAY BE FAIR TO SAY,
BETTER THINGS ARE TAKING PLACE, SUCH AS,
YOU MAY MEET SOME ONE TO SHARE A LITTLE TREET,
PEOPLE MAY BE MORE FRIENDLY, A FRIENDLY HELLO,
OR A QUIET SMILE ON THEIR FACE.
THIS MAY SUGGEST, PEOPLE ARE EASY GOING.
ON THE OTHER HAND, THE OPPOSITE SIDE,
ONE MAY HEAR MUSIC OR LOUND NOISE,
OR OTHER DISRUPTIONS, NOT BEING VERY
PLASANT TO THE EAR.
IN COMMON TERMS, WE MAY SEE A QUALITY OF BEING WORTHY,
ON THE SERIOUS SIDE OF THIS STREET.
IT MAY BE CALLED THE BETTER SIDE.
WHEN I WAS A CHILD, SO INNOCENT, MEEK AND MILD,
NOT FULLY UNDERSTANDING THE GIST OF IT ALL.
LATER IN LIFE I LEARNED, YES, THE BETTER SIDE

OTHER SIDE OF THE STREET (continued)

WHERE MANY PEOPLE MEET, OFFERED A MORE
DELICATE TASTE OF LIFE (IF YOU WILL)
YES, MY FRIENDS, AND I HAVE LEARNED
NUMEROUS ISSUES MAYBE EVEN
DEBATABLE IN OUR WORLD TODAY.
AS WE REMEMBER THE BETTER SIDE OF THE STREET,
PERHAPS, THE QUESTION REMAINS?
IS IT THE BETTER SIDE OF THE STREET?
OR NOW THE SUNNY SIDE OF THE STREET,
OF COURSE, LIFE TENDS TO CHANGE DAILY.
WE ALL SHARE THE COMMON GOOD,
ON BOTH SIDES OF THE STREET,
WHERE WE GREET AND MEET,
ON SUNNY DAYS AND SOME NOT SO SUNNY
(IN MY IPINION) WE SHALL RESPECT BOTH SIDES.

"SOME GOOD PEOPLE"

IN THESE TIMES OF BEING UNCERTAIN ABOUT LIFE,
I FOUND MYSELF, ONE DAY SCRAMBLEING MY WAY
TO A LINE AT THE LOCAL GROCERY STORE, JUST TO FIND THE ITEMS
I NEEDED AT THAT TIME.
BUT OH, THAT LINE, I THOUGHT TO MYSELF,
I WILL NEVER SERVIVE, THIS LINE OF PEOPLE,
MOVING THE SAME DIRECTION AS MYSELF.
AGAIN, IN THESE TIMES OF OUR CRISIS, I HAD STOOD IN MANY LINES,
FOR JUST A FEW ITEMS.
ON THIS PARTICULAR DAY, SUDDENLY I SAW A PERSON
WITH A WINNING SMILE COMING TOWARD ME,
ASKING ME IF SHE COULD HELP,
I RETURNED THE SMILE AND ANSWERED (YES).
ON THAT DAY, I KNEW MY PRAYERS HAD BEEN
ANSWERED.
I THANKED THE PERSON THAT HELPED
ME, AND MY COMPLETED THOUGHTS WERE
SOME GOOD PEOPLE, YET EXIST.
WHEN WE CARE, WE ARE WILLING TO SHARE.

"DIRECTION"

I CLEARLY REMEMBER, YEARS AGO, WHEN TRAVELING
ON A COUNTRY ROAD, WHEN ONE WOULD STOP AND ASK?
FOR THE DIRECTION, THEY WERE WANTING TO GO,
THEIR DESTINATION, IN OTHER WORDS,
BACK IN THE DAY THE ROADS WERE DUSTY, AND MADE
OF GRAVEL, DUST FLYING EVERYWHERE.
PEOPLE WOULD PLEASURE YOU BY SAYING,
(GO ON DOWN THIS ROAD UNTIL YOU COME TO A
FORK IN THE ROAD)
YOU WERE TO GO RIGHT OR LEFT)
TAKE YOUR CHOICE, DUST YET FLYING AS YOU GO
YOU JUST GO, GO, GO,
NOW YOU KNOW YOU (R) IN THE RIGHT DIRECTION,
WITH OUT ANY PURE PROTECTION.
GO ON UP AHEAD.
AND FINNALY (YOU) SHALL REACH YOUR DESTINATION.
DO NOT STRAY BEFORE THE END OF DAY.
AS THE OLDER GENERATION WOULD SAY,
(ON UP AHEAD).

"STANDING ALONE"

LOOKING AT THE WATERS WAY OUT ON THE SEA.
THE WAVES ARE BROAD AND VERY, VERY, HIGH.
HOWEVER, THEY ARE STARING BACK AT ME.
THEY TELL A LITTLE STORY I HAVE NEVER HEARD?
A PRAYER, A SONG, AND A PURPOSE, SUNG BY
A MOCKING BIRD.
ALLOW ME TO SHARE WITH YOU, WHAT THIS
IMAGE MEANS TO ME.
JUST THE PERFECT PICTURE, I TRULY NEED TO SEE.
AND IN MY THOUGHTS, ON THIS VERY SPECIAL DAY.
A PICTURE AND A VISION HAVE BEEN SHARD
WITH ME, IN A SPECTACULAR SORT OF WAY.
YOU SEE, IN THESE WATERS OF THIS ROARING SEA
THE WAVES APPEAR TO BE REFLECTING GENTLY
BACK AT ME, WHILE I AM STANDING ALONE.

"OUT STRETCHED HANDS"

Obviously, our needs are not yet met, we need
Out stretched hands to give us an opportunity
To proudly take our stand,
On numerous issues in demand, in our unstable
And precarious land.
Let us stop and think for a bit,
Our hopes and incomplete dreams
Are not yet, and what it may seem,
Where is our ambition, to play a part?
In certain situations, from the start.
We must put forth the effort together,
Everyone on stage has a part to play,
Anticipating our efforts shall stay
In place so dreams shall come true,
After we have completed our task
In things we make an attempt to do
The question is? How does it feel to take a step back?
Knowing we must continue on the track,
To make it to the finish line,
in attempt to figure it all out.
However, it is a demand for everyone to be ready for the next bout.
Perhaps, our future shall guild us to the next step,

OUT STRETCHED HANDS (CONTINUED)

Again, please do not attempt to make that bet
Because, we -r- not finished with our task quite yet!
But when our DREAMS begin to unfold,
We, the people must be strong and incredibly bold,
In our message and our GOAL.
(in other words)
There must be a beginning, as we know,
Because the BIBLE TELLS US SO.
And I may share in quote "IN THE BEGINNING GOD CREATED
HEAVENS AND THE EARTH"
"AS IN GENESIS—KING JAMES VERSION."
Now in my opinion, we have been privileged
To the HEAVENS AND THE EARTH
AS WE, ALL KNOW IT'S WORTH.
To our lives.
TO MY READERS: PLEASE STAY Focused, SAFE AND BLESSED.

"SHUT IN"

On today, everyone is shut in or second choice is shut down.
However, we have the ability to walk around.
Those having the strength, to endure this experience
Shall patiently wait to take that tour.
Yes, a tour of life once again, because this is not the end.
This is the year of 2020, and we shall rise once again
Now, if you are living, share this with a friend.

"DO NOT INFLICT PAIN"

No more whippings, no more whelps!
Oh, what a day I shall never forget!
Those old days are with me yet, and I, shall never forget.
Way back then, there was no way to cover them up!
One just, drank from that bitter old cup.
But oh, that pain, I had to take, as I remember
This was in sane. Oh, the pain.
I often have wondered was that whelp a reminder, just for me?
Not, to forget that day of anger, not made by me.
I had to accept, because I was a child, this to endure, made me,
So meek and mild.
I suppose, it did because today, when I think back in those
Old days, I weep in my soul and wonder why? I had to endure
That dreadful pain.
However, today my life is BRIGHT
And GOD has been with me.
I am here just to say, DO NOT INFLICT PAIN.

"RAINBOW IN WINTER"

COME WITH ME, I WANT TO SHARE WITH YOU,
MY PICTURE OF RAINBOW IN WINTER, AS WE OBSERVE,
NATURE ALL AROUND, WATCHING SNOWFLAKES,
TUMBLING DOWN, AS THEY SECURE THEM SELVES ON
THE SNOW FROZEN GROUND.
WONDER JUST HOW IT FEELS, WITH FREEZING TEMPERTURES
TO PROVE, IT IS SURREAL.
AS EACH FLAKE GLISTENS,
AS DIAMONDS AND JEWELS, SO RICH AND CLEAR.
INDICATES TO US, WINTER IS HERE.
NOT A SOUND TO BE HEARD, NOT EVEN A LITTLE MOCKING BIRD.
THESE SNOW FLAKES SO ELOQUENTLY GUILDED
BY THEIR OWN POWER AND STRENGTH,
TO LAND ON THEIR DESINATED SPACE, AS THEY GENTLY FALL
IN THEIR QUIET PLACE,
THE RAINBOW, CREATES ITS SPACE IN THE WONDERS OF THE SKY.

THESE SNOW FLAKES ARE SPECIAL IN FORMING THEIR PATTERN
BEFORE THEY LAND,
BUT SUDDENLY IN THE FAR DISTANT SKY, BEAUTIFUL
COLORS APPEAR PROVIDING A SENSE OF
SECURITY, HAPPINESS, STRENGTH, AND PEACE
IT APPEARS TO BE A RAINBOW IN THE SKY.

RAINBOW IN WINTER BOOK # 5 (CONTINUED)

DISPLAYING A VIEW FROM ON HIGH.
HOWEVER, THESE COLORS IN THE SKY
SHARE A STORY, ALL THEIR OWN,
TO REMIND A DREAMER, SUCH AS THIS, NO ONE SHALL
EVER BE ALONE.
BECAUSE, WITH SNOW FLAKES AND A RAIN BOW,
A TRUE PICTURE HAS BEEN DEVELOPED AND SHOWN.
ON THE OTHER HAND, IN AN INSTANT, THE RAIN BOW
SHALL DISAPPEAR, TO LEAVE THE MEMORY IN
THE MIND, SOMETHING MYSTERIOUS WAS HERE.
LET US NOT FORGET, THE SNOW FLAKES CONTINUE TO
FILTER DOWN, AS THEY GENTLY COVER THE ENTIRE GROUND.
TO MY READERS:
YOU SEE, A DREAM IS A JEWEL, YOU MAY KEEP IN YOUR MIND,
AS YOU SLEEP.
THIS RAINBOW APPEARED IN WINTER AS A GIFT
FOR YOU TO FOREVER KEEP.

"TIME OUT"

TAKE TIME OUT, JUST TO SAY?

DEAR LORD
GIVE ME THE WORDS TO SAY, ALLOW ME TO FOCUS,
AND NOT STRAY.
WHEN MY BURDENS APPEAR DIFFUCULT TO BEAR,
HELP ME TURN TO SOME ONE AND SHARE.
GIVE ME THE KNOWLEDGE, AND THE WORDS TO SAY,
SO I MAY BE COMFORTED ON THIS DAY.
I SEEM TO BE IN A FOREST OF DENIAL.
THANK YOU FOR YOUR HELP.

"DAYS OF SUN SHINE"

DAYS OF SUNSHINE IN MY HEART, WHERE ON EARTH,
DO I START?
WHEN, I AWAKE TO THE EARLY SUN, MY DAY
BEGINS WITH THE BRIGHTNESS FROM THE
RAYS OF THE SUN. I TEND TO LOOK ACROSS
THE SEA, AS THE WATERS GLISTEN BACK AT ME.
SAYING IT IS A WONDERFUL DAY, JUST WAITING FOR
TOMARROW.
YET NOT KNOWING WHAT TOMARROW SHALL
BRING MAYBE SUNSHINE OR A BIT OF RAIN.
THE QUESTION, I MAY ASK OF MY SELF, WITH IN
MY HEART, AGAIN TODAY! WHERE SHALL I START?
I ALSO MAY ASKED AND ANSWER TOO?
THINKING OF DIFFICULT MOMENTS
WHICH MAY CONTINUE, I AM ASKING,
HOW TO OVER COME? WHEN I THINK OF WHAT I HAVE?
OR WHAT I HAVE TO GIVE? MY ANSWER IS:
"LOVE"
AND DAYS OF SUN SHINE ALL IN ONE.

"REFLECTION FROM HEAVEN"

This page is dedicated to my readers:

If you can only imagine,
A REFLECTION FROM HEAVEN
I shall attempt to share with you my most recent experience.
On a very special day.
Recently, I decided to have a picture made, (of me).
So, I asked my son to perform the task for me.
When he finished, he had several pictures for me to choose from.
So, I thanked him.
On the next morning, again I decided to have them developed,
So I could frame them.
In the process of completion,
I begin to view them closely,
However, I quickly made my choice, but as I looked
More closely, I gently tossed one aside, not wanting it.
After a few seconds, something special happened:
And to my surprise, a source standing close to me,
Made a comment about the picture, I had tossed a side
The picture, had a reflection of the SUN in the background,
That being said, the source shared with me, and made the
Comment that "GOD WAS SHINNING DOWN ON ME,
AND TAKING CARE OF ME." (In reference to the picture.)

REFLECTION FROM HEAVEN (continued)

This is how the picture appeared to my source.
To recapture the picture, suddenly I became speechless,
And in that special moment, I did not know what to say.
Only this was a wonderful day.
This moment became a spiritual moment for me,
After hearing, the remark from my source.
In my next breath, I shared with my source,
Looking at this picture once again, it seems to be right.

Yes, the title of my next book of poetry,
Was revealed in this spiritual moment.
"REFLECTION FROM HEAVEN"
My experience on that day enlightened my sense of
Reality.
And I now believe, that when we push back certain things,
GOD is showing us exactly what he wants us to do.
And pay attention to his guidance.
I believe HE is showing us in his sign of time,
Allowing us to increase our FAITH in him.
The message for me on that day, was to share
With you the feeling of a brighter day ahead
And to increase our FAITH, on our daily journey.
I believe our lives reflect on the next GENERATION.

REFLECTION FROM HEAVEN (continued)

Giving them purpose for living and to expand their dreams.
As GOD shinned his sun rays on me, on that special day.

"SEE"

Today, we shall focus on what do you SEE?
Sometime people look at others, but do not see them.
For example: people do not see the inter heart of others,
Or the true expression on their face. I mean eye to eye contact,
For another example, their eyes may be showing
Happiness or sadness, start with their smile, on a sunny
Day, what does the picture have to say?
Or someone may have a frown, and suddenly looking down.
And a mere stranger, may asked, the question, how may I help you?
Today, in that moment, do not look away.
On the other hand, yes, we may look at them,
But perhaps not seeing them, eye to eye.
Now, wonder why?
In my opinion: eyes tell an interesting story,
Without much effort,
Suddenly, a sense of silence, to the unknown?
Feeling with in the heart and soul of others.
Most of the time, most stories, are told thru,
The expression on the face of others.
Yes, we may share looks, but the question yet remains?
What do we see?
We may wonder, how it is possible to look,

SEE (continued)

Yet unable, to see the total picture of others.
Some what a simple answer, may be?
Most of the time, our mind is focused on many other,
Situations, in life, too numerous to count!
For example, once again, we may see a DEEP BLUE SEA,
With the rippling of the waters, and waves bracing
Against each other, causing an even flow,
Across the sea shore, on the other side,
Enclosed by land, on the other hand, what do we see?
A beautiful DEEP BLUE SEA, for others to view,
In that catching moment, a story to be shared,
With the entire world.
Yet when we look at others, sometime our thoughts,
Are interacting with other issues, in our life.
So, today I choose to share with you
On tomorrow, when you look, please focus on the true
Picture, when you look at others, face to face.
You just may be of help to your
AMERICAN SISTERS AND YOUR BROTHERS.
When you are looking at (others).

"Show me love"

Create within me a touch, the feel, the thought
of perfect love, the privilege,
To hold, and never let go.
Just show me perfect love.
The smile, the gleam, the forever element of
this thing called love. Where is it, how may I find it?
Perhaps, the smile on your face, may lead me to the
Place where I may be surprised to find love.
I need to discover this thing called LOVE.
SOME ONE TO SHARE, SOME ONE TO CARE,
ABOUT MY MOST INTIMATE FEELINGS.
I NEED TO BE TAUGHT HOW TO LOVE,
AND HOW TO RECOGNIZE THE ELEMENTS
OF THE TRUE MEANING OF LOVE.
HOW SHALL WE KNOW? WILL OUR BODY GIVE US INDICATORS?
AS HOW TO PROCEED WITH THIS THING CALLED LOVE.
THE WARMTH FROM THE SOUL, MAYBE HIDING
AN INCREDIBLE SECRET, YET TO BE TOLD,
ABOUT TWO LOVERS.
PLEASE HOLD MY HAND
MY DARLING, AND GIVE ME LOVE TO FULLFILL
MY EMPTINESS, I WILL KNOW IF IT IS PURE, AND SPOTLESS
AS SILVER OR GOLD, BECAUSE YOU SHALL BE SHARING

Show me love (continued)

YOUR INNER SOUL WITH ME.
THE STARS ABOVE SHALL SHOW THAT INNTER LOVE SHINNING
DOWN FROM HEAVEN ABOVE.
THERE MAY BE A DELIGHTFULL FEELING OF PURE LOVE
IN THE MIDDLE OF A QUIET NIGHT,
ONLY WHEN THE PROPER APPOINTED TIME IS RIGHT.
ONE INTERESTING, THING, WE SHALL SHARE GOD'S
AMAZING LOVE ALWAYS, WITH OURS.

"SOUND"

LISTEN TO THE SOUND OF A BIRD, WHEN IT SOUNDS
SOME WHAT LIKE: CHIRP, CHIRP,
SOME TIME, WE SIMPLY IGNORE SOUND
SUCH AS WHEN LEAVES ARE HITTING THE GROUND,
YET THEY ARE FALLING DOWN.
MOST OF US JUST TAKE FOR GRANTED, BECAUSE
IT IS NATURE PLAYING THE PART, AND IT IS NATURAL
FOR US.
NOW LISTEN TO THE SOUND OF A PLAN IN THE AIR
ABOVE THE CLOUDS, THAT SOUND ATTRACKS OUR
ATTENTION FOR SOME STRANGE REASON.
EVERY THING HAS ITS SEASON.
LISTEN TO THE RAIN DROPS ON A QUIET NIGHT,
PITER PATTER ON THE ROOF TOP, WE SUDDENLY
DISCOVERY, IT IS THE RAIN DROPS, BUT WE JUST TAKE FOR
GRANTED THE SOUND, BECAUSE IT IS NATURAL.
NOW LISTEN TO THE SOUND OF BURNING WOOD,
AS IT TENDS TO CREATE A CRACKLING SOUND
TO OUR EARS.
THE SMELL OF SMOKE, NEARLY TAKING OUR BREATH
CAUSED BY THE WINDS, COMING FROM THE
NORTH, SOUTH, EAST, AND WEST

SOUND (continued)

AND BEFORE WE RECOGNIZE THE MOMENT, WE
HEAR THE SOUND OF FLATTERING WINGS, INVOLVED
IN THEIR OWN SPECIAL TIME AT HAND.
NOW IT IS TIME TO LISTEN TO THE SOUND OF
A SIREN, COMING DOWN A QUIET STREET,
BUT THIS SOUND GIVES US A SENSE OF
WHAT IS HAPPENING NOW? AND WE STOP!
TO LOOK UP, OR DOWN THE STREET,
TO OBSERVE THE INTER ACTION WITH OTHERS.
SOME TIME IT TAKES SOUND TO BRING PEOPLE
TOGETHER, NO MATTER WHAT THE WEATHER?
TAKE TIME OUT TO LISTEN TO THE TRAIN ON THE TRACK,
PROCEEDING FORWARD NOT TO RETURN COMING BACK
HOW EVER IT MAY GET OUR ATTENTION.
OTHER TIMES, WE MAY HEAR MUSIC IN THE AIR
AND SIMPLY WONDER, THE SOUND IS WHERE?
YES, ALL OF THESE THINGS PLAY AN IMPORTANT
CYCLE IN OUR DAILY LIFE.
BECAUSE IT IS A PART OF LIFE, WE MUST NOT IGNORE,
EACH DAY ALSO HAS ITS MOMENTS, AND MORE.
PERHAPS WE ARE A PART OF IT AS WELL.
I SUGGEST, TAKE TIME TO LISTEN TO THE SOUNDS
OF EACH DAY, COMIMG YOUR WAY.

A PANDEMIC EXPERIENCE---

AS WE EXPERIENCE THIS PANDEMIC IN 2020, 2021.
SO FAR WE, JOIN WITH OTHERS, TO ASSIST
WHERE EVER, WE ARE ABLE TO LEND A HELPING HAND.
WE ARE WITH CROWDS OF PEOPLE, NOT KNOWING JUST
WHAT TO DO? YET WE ARE WILLING TO PERFORM
THE TASK AT HAND.
FROM ONE DAY TO THE NEXT,
TRYING TO PERFORM OUR VERY BEST.
AT THIS TIME, WE MUST BE SOME DISTANCE APART,
BUT OUR DAILY TASK WILL NOT STOP.
WE MUST TRY TO SAVE LIFE AS WE SEE IT
AT THE TIME.
NO MATTER DAY OR NIGHT, WE MUST ATTEMPT TO
MAKE THINGS RIGHT TO SAVE A LIFE.
WE MAY ASK? WHERE DO WE START?
AND WHAT IS MY PART?
HOW EVER, WE KNOW WE MUST GO! TRY TO SAVE A LIFE.
SOME ONE'S MOTHER, DAD, SISTER OR BROTHER TOO
AND EVER GRAND PARENT AND FAMILY MEMBER
IN OUR CIRCLE IS HURTING WITH PAIN,
PRAYING AND HOPING THINGS SHALL
RETURN NORMAL ONCE AGAIN.

(PANDEMIC) CONTINUE

WE MAY MAKE A FEW STEPS BACK AND FORWARD
AND WE MAY FEEL SOMEWHAT OUT OF PLACE.
BUT NO MATTER WHAT? WE SHALL TRY
TO AVOID THE TEARS FLOWING FROM YOUR
EYES AND FACE.
SOON, WE PRAY THE PIECES OF THIS PUZZLE
SHALL DISAPPEAR SOME DAY.
WE SUDDENLY LOOK AROUND TO SEE, WHO IS
YET LOOKING AT ME.
AND MAYBE THINKING WHAT WILL BE, WILL BE.
ON THE OTHER HAND, WE SHARE A SMILE,
AND SHARE OUR LOVE WITH THAT PERSON
DOWN THE AISLE.
JUST REMEMBER, IN OUR THOUGHTS
WE MUST CONTINUE ON AND PERFORM
OUR BEST IN THIS PANDEMIC STROM.
BE SAFE, RESILIENT, AND COUNT YOUR BLESSING., ONE BY ONE.

"STANDING IN THE DOOR"

Standing in the door waiting on you,
Standing so calm and gently, thinking of what to do?
As I look down the street, again what do I see?

Many people laughing, and looking back at me.
I gently focus, on the kids in the streets,
As some are running fast in their bare feet.
Yet, I hear kids crying, while tears roll down their cheeks,
As they look around, trying to see people to meet.
On the other han**d**, some appear happy and gay
While others, continue to play.
But the story is plan and bold, here is a story to be told.
It is so obvious, their wants and their needs,
They are waiting on someone to bring them comfort,
And ease, remember to say thank you and please.
It is in their little hearts, and shows on their face,
This situation, is not the safe place to be,
While I stand waiting for you, so many things are
Obviously wrong, everyone is wondering, just
What they may contribute to the cause, to make things
Acceptable once again.

STANDING IN THE DOOR (continued)

Whatever may come their way, people are just thankful for
Breath on today.
They may just pray for hope and security on tomorrow
To create a new start, and delete to days' sorrow from
Their lonely HEART.
Watching others coming along, standing in their own
door way all alone.

YES, there is a story to be told, to other people in language,
Plain and bold.
If we walk away from the door, indeed there is plenty more
To see, so increase your love to others you know,
And add to your list, the unknowns, because they
Are waiting on you to think of
The unfortunate ones, such as the kids on the street in their bare feet,
New people you and I shall meet and greet.
I shall wait for you, standing in the door, no matter
How long it may take, my message is, hold on to life
And justify a reason for standing in the door.

"STAY AHEAD OF YOUR GAME"

Life is uncertain, not only today, but on most days.
Think ahead, and try to figure exactly what is in your way?
For beginners, you may not know, exactly what is ahead of you,
But, be ready to explore your options, from your point of view.
Question? what is old and what is new?
For you.
Just be ready to hold the world in your hands,
So, you are able to understand,
The complicated days ahead of you.
Some questions are without answers,
Not only for you, but for everyone.
We are unable to proceed forward, not knowing what is right or wrong.
At least that is every one's song.
For the most part, in our poor heart,
We some time wonder just where to simply start?
We must acquire, new ideals, new skills
New thoughts, and make new transitions in our thought process.
It is a new day, a new time, for everyone.
So, stay ahead of your game.
And things will not be the same,
Because you are aspired to create the change,

"STAY AHEAD OF YOUR GAME" (continued)

Everything is taking a new turn before our eyes,
We must have the ability to realize,
The change that is necessary in our world today.
There must be a new you and a new me,
And together, we shall see, a BETTER WORLD.
We are searching for a new future,
For every little boy and every little girl,
This is why, the search for a new world,
Shall become a reality.
TO MY READERS:
The time is now, a new day and a new way,
Is necessary,
Just remember to STAY AHEAD OF YOUR GAME.
Things shall not be the same,
In the END.

"STAY YOUNG"

HI MY FRIENDS, MY MESSAGE TODAY IS:
STAY YOUNG, WHILE LIVING AND GROWING OLDER,
DO NOT ALLOW TRIALS AND TRIBULATIONS
TO INTERFERE WITH YOU LIVING, AND ENJOYING
LIFE, AND WHAT IT MAY OFFER YOU,
AT BEST.
SOME TIME WE THINK DIFFERENTLY
ABOUT ISSUES IN LIFE, AND HOW TO DEAL WITH THEM.
ON THE OTHER HAND, WE MUST ATTEMPT,
TO MAKE AN EFFORT TO SUCCEED.
USE NEW IDEALS AND TECHNIQUES TO MEET OUR NEED.
OUR PRESENT WORLD IS SO ADVANCED,
WHEN OPPORTUNITY COMES, WE MUST TAKE A CHANCE,
AND MOVE FORWARD WITH OUR PURPOSE.
HOW EVER, WE MUST STAY YOUNG,
AS WE GROW "OLD"
SO OUR STORIES SHALL CONTINUE TO BE TOLD,
IN LANUAGE PLAIN AND BOLD.

"A SPECIAL LITTLE BIRD"

I REMEMBER ONE DAY, GIVING A WARM WELCOME
TO A VISITOR, IT HAPPEN TO BE A LITTLE BIRD,
AS I SAT WAITING FOR A KNOCK AT THE DOOR,
TO MY SURPRISE I, HEARD A STRANGE SOUND,
ON THE GROUND, IT WAS A LITTLE BIRD,
TRYING TO CAPTURE MY ATTENTION.
IMMEDIATELY AS I LOOKED AROUND, IT WAS
PECKING ON THE GROUND, WAITING TO BE FOUND,
WHEN IT BEGIN TO FLUTTER, ITS WINGS,
THEY PRODUCED A PLEASANT SOUND,
I COULD HAVE ADDED A LITTLE CHEERFUL SONG,
TO MAKE THINGS GO RIGHT, AND NOT ENDING UP WRONG,
THIS HAPPY LITTLE BIRD BROUGHT JOY
TO MY HEART, RIGHT FROM THE VERY START.

"A SLIPPERY PATH WAY"

FIRST OF ALL, TRY TO IMAGENE A SLIPPERY PATH,
WHEN YOU MAY BE WALKING,
WE MAY THINK OF THE PURE ELEMENTS OF THE WEATHER,
SUCH AS WATER, RAIN, ICE, SNOW, WIND,
ROCKS, MUD SLIDE, A LOST FOREST, THAT HAS NO END, NEVER
BEEN DISCOVERED, OR UNCOVERED BY ANY ONE.
BY NOW YOU HAVE THE IDEA, (RIGHT?)
ALL OF THESE INTERUPTIONS, SOME TIME INTERFERE
WITH OUR THINKING PROCESS OF TRYING
TO TRAVEL ON A SLIPPERY PATH.
REMEMBER, WE HAVE NO OTHER OPTIONS AT THIS TIME,
BUT WE ARE TRYING TO AVOID A FALL.
SUCH IS LIFE, NOT TO FALL. SO ONE MUST
FOCUS ON YOUR OBSERVATION, AS TO WHAT IS
IN OR ON YOUR PATH.
WHY IS IT NOT CLEAR?
AND WHY ARE OBSTICLES YET HERE?
SO WE NEED TO EVALUATE THE TRUE SITUATION,
TRYING TO BALANCE YOUR STEPS AS YOU MAY
CONTINUE, BUT YOU HAVE NOT REACHED YOUR
SURPRISE PATH WAY YET, BUT IF ANY
OF THESE APPARENT REASONS (R) AT FAULT,

THE SLIPPERY PATH (continued)

YOU MUST TRY TO BALANCE YOUR STEPS, AS YOU GO.
AND YOU SHALL SOON KNOW,
YOU MUST CHOOSE A PATH STRAIGHT AND SMOOTH,
A ROUTE, FOR YOU, NOT TO LOOSE.
PLEASE TAKE TIME TO THINK, BECAUSE LIFE IS
GONE IN A BLINK.

"DAYS, NOT CLEAR"

IN THESE TIMES, WE ARE PRAYING, HOPING, AND WONDERING
ABOUT TOMARROW? BECAUSE TODAY IS NOT CLEAR
TO US.
AND TOMARROW IS AN UNKNOWN?
IT MAY BE CLOUDY TOO.
SO, PUT ON YOUR THINKING CAP, AND DETERMINE
JUST WHAT STEP TO TAKE?
OR WHAT MOVE TO MAKE?
WE ALL HAVE DEVELOPED A LITTLE FEAR,
BECAUSE A DOUBTFULL TIME IS NEAR.
(IN MY OPINION)
JUST LIVE TODAY, AND DO NOT TAKE AWAY,
THE TOOLS OF WHAT MAY WORK FOR TOMARROW.

"GRAB LIFE"

STOP IN YOUR TRACKS, TAKE ONE STEP FORWARD
BUT NOT BACK.
GRAB A LEAF, GRAB A STRAW, CRAB A ROCK,
GRAB A BLADE OF GRASS, GRAB A WAVE ON THE OCEAN SIDE,
HOLD IT TIGHT, WITH ALL YOUR MIGHT,
EVEN IN THE STILLNESS OF THE NIGHT,
GRAB A STAR, WHERE EVER YOU (R).
YOU MAY SOON DISCOVER, WHOM YOU REALLY ARE?
GRAB A BREATH OF THE WIND, HOLD ON,
BECAUSE THE FUTURE HAS NO END.
GRAB A SNOW BALL BEFORE IT HITS THE FROZEN GROUND,
HOLD IT IN YOUR HAND, FOR AS LONG AS YOU CAN,
GRAB THE SUN RAYS IN THE MIDDLE OF ANY DAY,
IT JUST MAY BE YOUR FUTURE, COMING
YOUR WAY.
GRAB A RAIN DROP COMING YOUR WAY, BEFORE
IT HITS THE ROOF TOP, THAT IS WHEN IT WILL STOP.
GRAB THE MIST OF A SUMMER NIGHT, BEFORE
THE MORNING SUN BRINGS YOU LIGHT.
GRAB THE DEW IN THE EARLY MORN,
BEFORE, THE NEXT LITTLE BABY IS BORN.

GRAB LIFE (continued)

THIS MAY GIVE THEM LIFE TO SHARE, AND A FUTURE
DREAM UNSEEN.
DEPENDING ON WHAT YOU WANT, MAY DEPEND ON
WHAT YOU GRAB AT YOUR SPECIAL TIME.
AND DEPENDING ON WHAT YOUR SCIENCE DIRECTS
YOUR ABILITIES TO PERFORM IN YOUR OWN
UNIQUE WORLD.
JUST REMEMBER, TAKE TIME TO GRAB SOMETHING,
BEFORE IT IS TO LATE.
(THIS WORLD GIVES, BUT ALSO TAKES)

"STAYING IN A ONE ROOM SHACK"

THIS LITTLE STORY BEGINS LIKE THIS:
JUST TO STAY IN A ONE ROOM SHACK,
NEVER TO STOP, TAKE A BREATH, OR LOOK BACK,
BECAUSE EVERY THING IN IT WAS SQUEEZED
BACK TO BACK.
FOR EXAMPLE, A CEARL BOWL, NEXT TO A SPOON,
SITTING ON A TABLE UNTIL LUNCH AT NOON.
AND A BOWL OF SOUP THAT TASTE SO GOOD,
IT WAS NOT THE BEST NUTRITION, AT THE TIME, BUT IT
FILLED THE EMPTYNESS, A GLASS OF COLD
WATER, WITH OUT ANY ICE,
AND THINKING A CAN OF SODA COULD BE NICE.
THINKING TOO, A GOOD OLD HOT APPLE PIE,
I COULD IMAGENE, SEEING WITH ONE EYE.
WOULD HIT THE SPOT, BUT NO MONEY TO BUY?
SO NOW A LITTLE COOKIE WILL HAVE TO DO
AND ONLY ONE, CERTAINLY NOT TWO. AND
IN THAT LITTLE ONE ROOM SHACK,
TAKING TIME TO SEE THE UGLY LITTLE CRACKS.
BUT, NOW OVER THE YEARS, OF SO LONG AGO,
IT SERVES AS A REMINDER, THAT I KNOW.
AND NOW WHEN I WANT A TREET, AND ENJOY
SOMETHING DELICIOUS TO EAT.

"STAYING IN A ONE ROOM SHACK BOOK # 5 CONTINUED.

THINKING OF THOSE DAYS, MADE ME HUMBLE AND
NOT FORGETING THE DAYS OF LESS, SOME TIME
BRINGING OUT THE BEST IN ALL OF HUMAN NATURE.
A NEW LIFE, NOW TO ENJOY, TO EVERY LITTLE GIRL AND BOY.
NOW SHARING THE BEST BUT HAVING BEEN,
THRU THE UNFORTUNATE TIMES,
INSPIRES OUR PURPOSE AND GIVES US AMBITION
TO PERFORM OUR BEST AS THE HUMAN RACE.
BETTER DAYS ARE NOW IN THE FUTURE,
BUT HAVING THE OLD DAYS TO REMEMBER,
AND NEVER TO FORGET
(THE LITTLE ONE ROOM SHACK)
IT GIVES ONE STRENGTH TO CARRY ON.
TO MY READERS: BE PRODUCTIVE IN YOUR LIVING
AND DO NOT FORGET YOUR FAITHFULL GIVING.
(SHARING WITH OTHERS.)

"TEAR DROPS IN MY COFFEE"

ONE SPECIAL MORNING, WHEN I WAS PREPARING MY COFFEE,
Suddenly a tear drop fell into my coffee cup.
Of course, I was crying, because you were on my mind.
And I suddenly wondered why?
But on the other hand, some time we have reason to cry,
I stopped for a moment, and begin to pray,
And this is what a small still voice began to say,
GOD SHALL DIRECT YOUR PATH ON TODAY.
In that exciting moment, I felt better.
Because I want your journey to be a pleasant one.
Life is not always pleasant, but you/we must
Have dreams in our heart and make them come true,
If possible.
We all must ask GOD to help us define our direction
In life.
And when we accomplish one step at a time,
Other steps shall be made easy.
You shall see.
Your answers will become clear as day,
In a spectacular way just for you.
Now perhaps I shall enjoy my cup of COFFEE
With my tear drops adding a special taste while thinking of you.

"TEARS IN MY COFFEE"

When I awakened this morning, with tears in my eyes,
As I attempted to make my coffee,
I looked down and discovered a tear drop,
fell into my coffee.
As I proceeded, a special person was on my mind,
But some time we must take time to cry.
I suddenly stopped, for a moment, and asked GOD,
To direct your path, on today.
Because, I want your journey to forever last.
In a good way.
As I remember, you have experienced many
Bad days, in your time.
It is time for some good times to be in your life,
Again, that is in my opinion.
I have asked GOD to give you the answer,
Before the end of day?
So, you shall know in your heart,
The beginning of a new and perfect start.
Some time, we meet others in our life,

TEARS IN MY COFFEE (cont.)

Many years ago, and at the time, the question is,
What direction (you) must go?
You may think and think again, what is
the problem?
Again, you may need that change in your life,
But fail to admit the grief and strife.
But, as for you, stop and take things slow,
so, you have time to think, and decide,
how and where you must go?
You shall recognize the change for you.
If I may add, we all have been a teen, only trying
To find our way?
But in my opinion,
Young adults, are trying to DEFINE THEIR WAY.
So, we must ask GOD to help us DEFINE?
What in life is our own?
Some time, we must change our way of thinking
And live for (us).
When our hearts, tell us the answer,

TEARS IN MY COFFEE (cont.)

It is then, we discover, the problem is (us)?

We asked GOD to continue to be with us, and
Direct our unknown path.
And give us a life, that will forever last.
And now, to my READERS:
I shall drink my cup of coffee with,
My tears.

"THE BIG PICTURE"

You and I, are traveling on this rough and rocky road together.
Some days, we see dust, winds, fog and sometime a bit
Of sunshine to brighten our view, providing us
With a sense, of courage to continue on our journey.
Suddenly, the dust becomes so heavy, blocking our way,
Making it impossible to see the people in front of us.
But we refuse to give up our challenge, because they are traveling too.
Some people are walking slow, however, they have the courage to go.
One thing we all know; this is a dusty road.
As we travel, suddenly, the dust disappears and we see the
Sunshine, peaking thru, this road has become smooth as
A ribbon, and straight as a path without any detours ahead.
This road is straight and long, makes us wonder,
What has gone wrong, if anything?
We now see beautiful flowers, along the way, greeting
Us on the right and the life.
The colors are a sight to see, we wonder how this could even be.
Without a doubt, we continue to travel this mysterious road ahead.
Surprisingly, no one has asked where this road shall lead us?
We just continue on.

THE BIG PICTURE) continued

At this time, no one really cares!
As long, as we stay together and just move ahead.
Now, we view the beautiful trees,
Forming an arch directly over our head,

To supply a shelter for all to share, leaving our burdens,
No more to bare.

Suddenly, when we look again, we see a beautiful
Blue sky, a heavenly blue, if you can imagine,
A HEAVENLY BLUE?
This site is breath taking, in our own mind.
As we continue to travel this mysterious road.
No one has mention of becoming sick, or tired!
Or even the thirst for water.
Everyone is just walking and talking.
As we travel this road.
We feel bold, confident, and free.
Because, we are together, as one.
We all are striving for the same,
A good and faithful life, we must lead,
Others may join us in the END. So all shall accomplish an enormous WIN.

"THE BIG PICTURE"

You and I, are traveling on this rough and rocky road together.
Some days, we see dust, winds, fog and sometime a bit
Of sunshine to brighten our view, providing us
With a sense, of courage to continue on our journey.
Suddenly, the dust becomes so heavy, blocking our way,
Making it impossible to see the people in front of us.
But we refuse to give up our challenge, because they are traveling too.
Some people are walking slow; however, they have the courage to go.
But one thing we all know.

"THE CATCH FOR TODAY"

Ten steps ahead, but twenty steps behind.

The faster I go; it appears to be a bit slow.

The harder I plan, the lesser I have the ability to expand.

The higher, I fly, the higher the sky.
The closer I reach, things seem to be a long way off,
And out of my view.

Things are moving, as I go, sometime fast and sometime slow.
I can't obviously catch up with myself,
There is a problem (right)?
I just cannot figure it out, this equation is so difficult,
I need help, and maybe just maybe that is the missing part,
IT IS ME!

THE FLYING SAUCER (OR U F O) EXPERIENCE

IN MY EARLY DAYS, AT THE AGE OF 17 YEARS OLD.
I SAW AN OBJECT, THAT APPEARED TO ME,
AS A FLYING SAUCER, THAT IS WHAT I THOUGHT
AT THE TIME, IN MY YOUNG MIND.
THERE WAS THIS HUGE ROUND WHITE,
OBJECT FLYING OVER HEAD, AS I WAS STANDING,
IN THE MIDDLE OF AN OPEN FIELD, IN THE
DESERTED COUNTRY SIDE, AS BEST I CAN DESCRIBE.
LOOKING UP IN DISMAY, I BECAME MESMERIZED
IN THE MOMENT, SO I BEGIN TO RUN, PUTTING
MY EFFORTS INTO ACTION MOOD.
I WAS THINGING AT THE TIME, I WAS ABLE TO,
FOLLOW THE DIRECTION OF THIS FLYING OBJECT.
BUT NOT SO, IT CONTINUED UNTIL IT WAS
OUT OF MY SIGHT,
I IMMEDIATELY, FOUND SOME FRIENDS, TO SHARE
MY EXPERIENCE WITH THEM, BEING KIDS,
OF COURSE, WE WERE EXCITED AT THE TIME.
WE BEGIN TO WALK TOWARD A WOODED AREA,
THINKING AT THE TIME, WE COULD DISCOVER THIS
UNKNOWN OBJECT.
AGAIN, THINKING AT THE TIME, WE COULD SEEK AND FIND,

THE FLYING SAUCER (continued)

THIS UNKNOWN INCREDIBLE OBJECT.
BUT TO OUR SURPRISE, WE WERE NOT WISE
ENOUGH TO THINK OF THE REALITY,
OF THIS EXPERIENCE.
WE WERE THINKING IT HAD LANDED ON THE GROUND.
HOW EVER THIS OBJECT WAS NOT SEEN OR
FOUND IN THE WOODS OR BY THE STREAMS,
IN OUR AREA, AT THAT TIME IN THE EARLY 1960'S.
I SHALL NEVER FORGET THIS ONE EXCITING EXPERIENCE,
IN MY LIFE, IT CAUSED ME TO BECOME MORE,
INTERESTED IN THE SCIENCE WORLD AND SPACE.

INNER FEELINGS

WE, SHALL START BY ASKING A QUESTION?
HOW WE MUST VIEW OUR FEELINGS, FROM THE HEART?
BEGINNING WITH OUR THINKING PROCESS? (ECT.)
HOW DO WE DEAL WITH OUR FEELINGS?
OUR EMOTIONS?
IT IS A PART OF LIFE, WE SOME TIME KEEP SECRET,
HOW EVER WE MAY NEED A FRIEND, A FAMILY MEMBER,
SOME ONE WE LOVE AND TRUST,
AFTER ALL IT IS OUR FEELINGS
DEPENDING ON THE CIRCUMSTANCES,
AND RELATIONSHIP WITH OTHERS.
DO WE USE OUR FEELINGS AS A CONNERSTONE?
IN OUR LIFE, OR A BUILDING BLOCK ON THE
FOUNDATION AS WE GROW FROM DAY TO DAY IN OUR LIFE.
(IN MY OPINION) SHARING WITH YOU.
LIFE IS SO SIGNIFICATE TO US, AS A MORTAR IS TO CLAY,
WE NEED TO BE MOLDED INTO THE FINAL PRODUCT.
THUS, BRINGING A SENSE OF VALUE TO US AS PEOPLE,
AT THE SAME TIME, WE NEED TO LEARN HOW,
TO DEVELOP OUR FEELINGS AND
EMOTIONS. AS PARENTS, WE MUST MAKE AN
ATTEMPT TO MOLD OUR CHILDREN, INTO

INNER FEELINGS (continued)

A JEWEL OF WORTH, SO THEIR GENERATION WILL BECOME
A LIFE TIME OF PEACE, JOY, AND HAPPINESS.
IN THEIR FUTURE LIFE, MAKING A BETTER WORLD,
TO CREATE A SPARK OF LIGHT,
TO ELECTRIFY THE ENTIRE WORLD.
BEGINNING WITH OUR TRUE FEELINGS AND
EMOTIONS.

"THE MOUNTAINS"

I see the mountain tops, but they are mountain peaks too,
And as I walk, they appear to me, as peaks, I am
Unable to reach.
The peaks appear to me as an up and down road
That never ends and winding curves that never bend.
The horizon is beyond compare, only people like me
Wish I could be there.
Your peaks, are the first to see the brightness
Of the sun.
As it rises, it whispers softly to you, I shall see you
At the end of day.
But before then, I have many things to say.
Such as:
I am on my way to discover your courage, your joy,
And your laughter, I also must add, your
Peaks are freighting to see, at least they are for me.
Now, I wonder if I will ever make it there on my adventure,
To see you.
I am so far away from you, I think each step
I attempt to make; it will equal an entire day.

I just realize, this journey is so long and difficult,

MOUNTAINS (cont.)

I may not have the strength to undertake,
Again, I must keep traveling toward your high peaks, (mountain top)
So, I may share my own skills with you.
I have decided to stop and pray for strength
To make me strong, and then wonder what?
Could possibly go wrong?
Again, numerous issues, may arise,
Before I make it to your side.
But I am moving gently as I go,
It seems to me; I am moving slow.
I refuse to give up, I shall drink from this bitter cup.
It may get sweeter as I continue my journey.
When I arrive, I desire to share with you,
The precious moments, I will have experienced
On this journey of trial and tribulations.
I stop and think, I must journey on.
To accomplish my goal and see it thru.
When I finally reach you, and your peaks,
I will rejoice, and be happy we shall meet.
I also shall share, my respect, kindness, grace, and love.
Because, by then you will have taught me a lesson from above.

MOUNTAINS (cont.)

Well learned.

And that lesson is:
That life's struggles, discontent, and patience
To endure, shall in the end, offers a payment,
That cannot be spent, it is worth holding onto
Forever!
Because this is your own life.
Be strong, be safe, take care, because we all are
Striving for the BEST LIFE WE are able to enjoy.

THE WORLD WE ONCE KNEW

When I reflect back on the world, I once knew
For example, home, family, and old friends.
I cannot forget the working profession too.
It was the most important vision that kept us going.
And that was why we do the things we do.
We once could walk, run, and play, but today
We are only able to say hello to our friends and neighbors.
Yes, this is the world we once knew.
Everyone is frightened now, because we know not what to think.
We, dare not to blink an eye.
Not knowing the real reason why?
We are informed, there is an unknown
Over taking the entire glob.
The world we once knew.
We do not have an answer now, the who, what, when, or where?
However, we are trying to hang in there.
Life is now, like a merry go round,
And it is not slowing down. We, only hope and pray for an answer soon.
So, in time we are able to fly to the moon.
This mysterious something?? Has been named
COVID-19
Daily, we hear, lives are being lost, we must keep the faith.

Continued: the world we once knew

We must hold on, and not let go, because as we live from day to day,
    We will find our way, and learn how to really pray.
        Our prayers are needed, one by one,
          Until we clearly see this battle won.,

"thinking inside OUT"

OUTSIDE, LOOKING IN OR IT COULD BE
INSIDE LOOKING OUT.
"QUIZ FOR THE WHIZ"
SO WE SHALL START BY SAYING,
THE EXCITEMENT OF BEING ON THE
OUT SIDE LOOKING IN OR IS THERE A POSSIBILITY?
OF ON THE INSIDE LOOKING OUT.
SOME TIME PEOPLE ARE SEEN AS TWO PARALLEL LINES,
BEING SIDE BY SIDE, BUT ALLOWING THE SAME DISTANCE
APART. TRUE ON ANOTHER NOTE,
WE MAY APPEAR TO BE TOGETHER,
YET SO FAR APART. AS OUR ATTEMPT IS MADE,
LET US PRETEND, WHAT WE ARE NOT!
I AM ON THE IN SIDE LOOKING OUT,
AND I VISION MANY THINGS ON THE OTHER SIDE,
IN MY IMAGINATION SUCH AS:
IMAGES OF TREES, AND FIELDS OF GREENERY,
ADDING A SPECTACULAR SCENERY, IN MY VIEW,
FEATURES OF A DISTANT LAND SCAPE,
NOT YET DISCOVERED.
YES, I AM INSIDE LOOKING (OUT).
NOW ON THE OTHER HAND, LET US ATTEMPT TO SAY

(THE OUT SIDE LOOKING IN)
SOME TIME IN OUR MIND, WE ASSUME THINGS ARE SEEN
IN A DIFFERENT PERSPECTIVE.
THINGS MAY APPEAR TO BE GLAMOROUS,
AND MORE APPEALING TO US, BECAUSE WE ARE ANXIOUS
TO SEE WHAT IS DIFFERENT THAN IN OUR MIND SET.
OUR ANTICIPATION IS RUNNING AWAY.
BUT NOT TO STAY.
NOW LET US ASSUME: YOU AND I ARE THE SAME
DISTANCE APART, ONLY NOW WE HAVE A
SIGNIFICANT NEW START, (IN OTHER WORDS)
WE OBSERVE DIFFERENT THINGS ON BOTH SIDES,
FOR EXAMPLE, (OUT SIDE LOOKING IN)
AND (INSIDE LOOKING OUT).
NOW THE QUESTION REMAINS?
WHAT HAVE WE LEARNED?
IN OUR OBSERVATION AND OUR PARTICIPATION.
WE CAN NOT ASSUME ANY THING, WE MUST
SEE IT TO BELIEVE IT, AND THEN SOME TIME THERE MAY BE
DOUBT, A FEELING OF UNCERTAINTY.
THANKS FOR YOUR TIME.
THE PLEASURE IS MINE.

"CHALLENGE"

LIFE IN MY OPINION, BEGINS WITH THE FIRST CHALLENGE,
IT BEGINS AT BIRTH, YES WHEN A BABY IS BORN,
AND TAKES THAT FIRST BREATH,
LIFE BEGINS, JUST TO HAVE THE ABILITY TO BREATH
IN AND OUT.
WE HOPE AND PRAY, EVERY DAY COULD BE THE SAME,
BUT NO, THAT IS NOT SO.
CHALLENGES ARE WITH US EVERY DAY,
AND WE MUST LEARN HOW TO DEAL WITH THEM
DAY BY DAY IN OUR OWN UNIQUE SORT OF WAY.
LESSONS TO LEARN, AND LESSONS TO TEACH,
PART OF WHAT MAKES LIFE UNIQUE.

"THIS IS A SHORT STORY"

A LITTLE BURNED SHACK

The story begins like this:
I know how it feels to respectfully live in a little burned shack,
And on this particular day, I remember, coming out the door,
Holding my school books in my hand, walking and never looking back,
Yes, on my way to school. This was my daily chore.
And if I may add, I was speaking to every one along the way.
While others were skipping, jumping, and running all around me,
As I smiled at each and every one on that day.
My smile of course, was a free gift, I offered to everyone.
And knowing I may see them again someday,
Traveling the opposite way.
But, at the end of that day, my heart gently answers,
Saying, it shall be ok!
After, the school day was over, and I begin to
Walk back to that little burned shack,
Again, my brave heart, telling me, to be strong,
As I make tiny steps along.
This experience was just for me to gracefully see,
My journey ahead shall be a shining star.
And for me to create a wonderful world of my own,

A LITTLE BURNED SHACK (continued)

But, never forget the memories of the little burned shack.
Of course, it was the beginning of a real future for me.
So, I am sharing with my readers,
No matter, how unfortunate the situation may be,
Just keep in your memory bank, the days
That were meant to be for you and for me.
In my case, it was the LITTLE BURNED SHACK,
THAT BROUGHT ME BACK, TO REALITY,
Creating within me a desire to conquer my dreams.
And make a better WORLD for me and others,
As they travel in this WORLD OF UNKNOWN ADVENTURE.
I often think of the:
LITTLE BURNED SHACK, many years ago.
However, I thank GOD, FOR THE experience and the memory
I shall for ever know.

"THIS PAGE IS FOR MY READERS"

Please take time to enjoy this page, so put your
Thinking cap on.
And choose one or more of the following words,
To use in your daily life, to help someone,
Who is having a struggle, just to make it to the end of the day?
Please, notice these words begin with the letter (R).

REDEEM

REDREAM

RENEW

REPLISHISH

RESPOND

RESTORE

REPLY

RESPECT

REPLAY

REPLACE

RESET

RESPOND

REBUILD

RESPSIBILITY

RE-INFORCE

REPEAT

FOR MY READERS (continued)

Now my friends, take time to RELAX,
And renew your strength in the LORD.
Have a good day with your chore of READING.

"TID BIT FOR TODAY"

I THINK, TO LIVE IS TO SUFFER THE PAIN,
HOWEVER, ON THE OTHER HAND,
TO SURVIVE IS TO FIND THE MEANING OF
SUFFERING AND WE ALL SHALL EXPERIENCE
PAIN AND SUFFERING, IN OUR LIVE TIME.
HAVE A HAPPY AND GLORIOUS DAY.

"A TID BIT FOR TODAY"

I believe GOD speaks to us, in ways,
We may not understand, he shows us a sign,
Unknown to our ability to
Comprehend.

Try to live life to the fullest each and every day,
Stay safe and blessed, and do not for get
To PRAY.
"LOVE"
Love means, no sorrow for tomorrow, always
Live for hope.
Love moving the clouds a little higher,
To allow sun shine into our heart.
Some time, we may use our imagination to create
Our own dream to mankind.

"TIME"

Hello readers, it is time to think about TIME.
In my opinion, we do not have time to wait on time, do we understand
The meaning of TIME?
"The indefinite continued progress of existence and events,
In the past, present, and future regarded,
As a whole (per dictionary)."
Question is, how do we think of (time)?
Well, we think as in: minutes, seconds, hours, days, weeks, months,
Years, centuries, etc.
Sometime people do not place value in TIME.
Such as in our everyday life.
Just think, if we were able to extend TIME.
How could we take advantage of this option?
If it were possible.
And some time we, think in our mind, if we had the ability
To turn back the hands of TIME.
In our own thinking, what could we have done differently?
And how we could make a transition in our life, to help others
Please, take TIME to make a change in your life,
For a BETTER world tomorrow.
And I say to you, THANKS FOR YOUR TIME.

"TURN AROUND"

Turn around, nothing seems to be headed in the right direction,
In these days and times. And people are asking the
Question, what is going on?
Nothing is turning out right, people are sobbing, in the
Darkest hour of the night. Tossing and turning, on the left and the right.
Suddenly, we stop, and begin to pray, saying,
HEAVENLY FATHER!
Please show us the way.
Where do we go, and what do we say?
What shall we do to make a new start?

We are here to construct a blend.
A blend that shall never fail.
And a blend that shall only prevail.
We, as people, need to be victorious, after our blending, has
Been accomplished and has entered into our hearts,
Then we shall mend, the vacant space in our hearts forever.

UPS AND DOWNS

FOR EVER UP, THERE IS A DOWN

FOR EVERY LAUGH, THERE IS A FROWN,
FOR EVER HIGH, THERE IS A LOW,
AND SOME TIME, WE KNOW, WE MUST GO!
JUST WANT YOU TO KNOW, THERE IS
A HIGH COMING BY:
TO OFFER YOU, HOPE FAITH, COURAGE, DIGNITY,
SELF WORTH, PROSPERITY, PEACE, GRACE, LOVE.
AS IN QUOTE" JAMES: 4:6 KING JAMES VERSION
BUT HE GIVENTH MORE GRACE WHEREFORE, HE
SAITH, GOD RESISTETH, THE PROUD, BUT GIVETH
GRACE UNTO THE HUMBLE."
LET US REMEMBER TO DRAW NEAR TO GOD.
IN THE TIME HE HAS GIVEN US.

www.ingramcontent.com/pod-product-compliance
Lightning Source LLC
Chambersburg PA
CBHW061200070526
44579CB00009B/77